~~~~ ~~~~~ — Happy Birth'
hope you like this special
+ poems, drawn + written th
a lady from Pangbourne.... perhaps you'll
want to keep it for your children, + grand-
children (?!) Lots of love
~~~~ ~~, ~~~~ ~~~, ~~~~ + ~~~~

Ann Emmons

P.S.... who knows, in a few years time
Andrew Lloyd Webber may do a musical based
on this book, called "Mice"!

The Mice of Lardon Hill

Published by Wayfarer Books, Pangbourne, Berkshire.

Produced by Ridgeway Press, Pangbourne, Berkshire.

(c) 1993 Text and illustrations by Ann Emmons
Vignettes by Jean Smith

First published in Great Britain 1993
by Wayfarer Books, Pangbourne, Berkshire.

No part of this book may be reproduced in any form without
permission from the publisher, except for the quotation of brief passages of review.

ISBN 0 9521663 0 5

To Jean, Richard and Annie

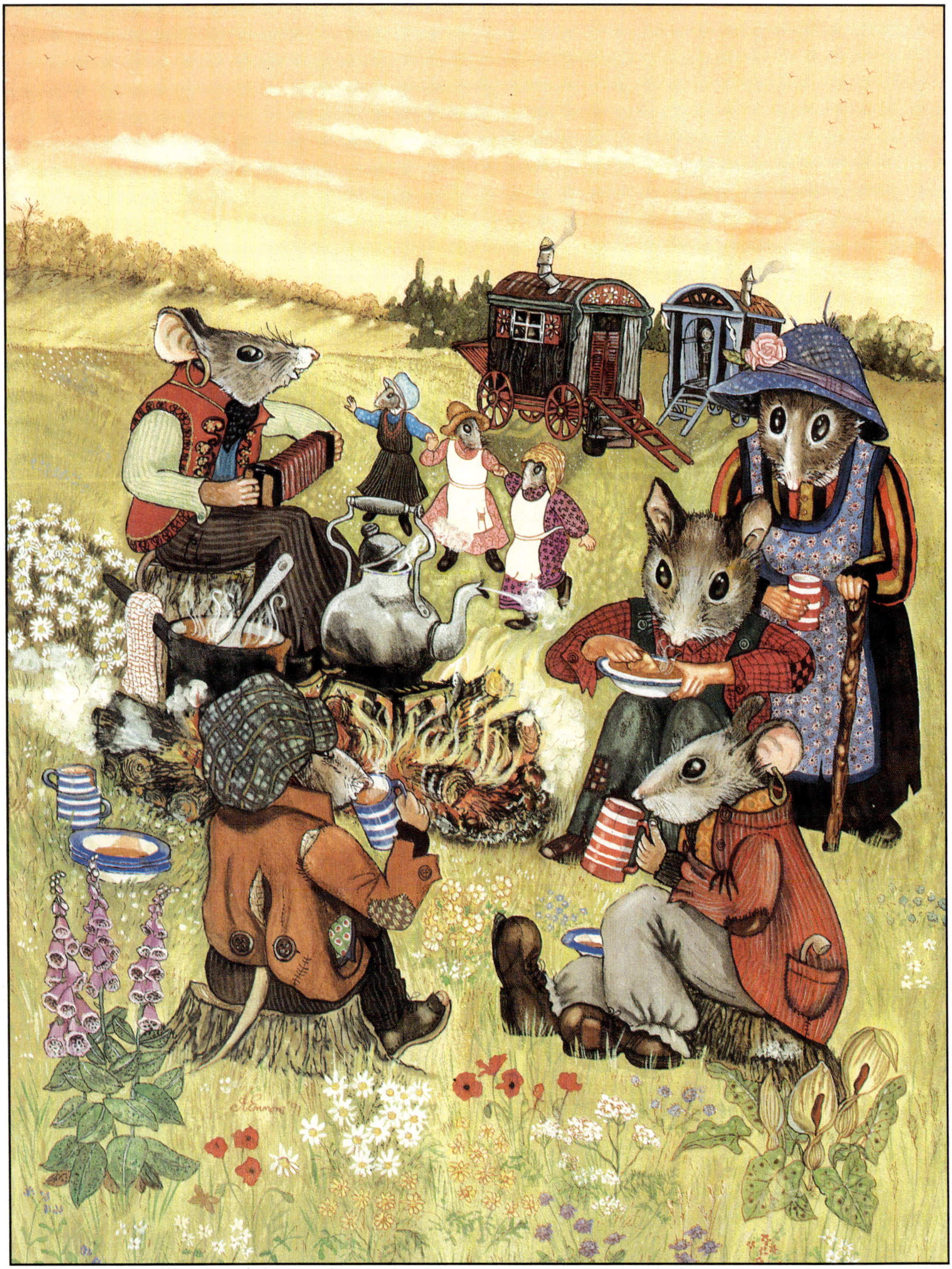

The Mice of Lardon Hill

A TREASURY OF POEMS

WRITTEN AND ILLUSTRATED
BY
ANN EMMONS

WITH VIGNETTES
BY
JEAN SMITH

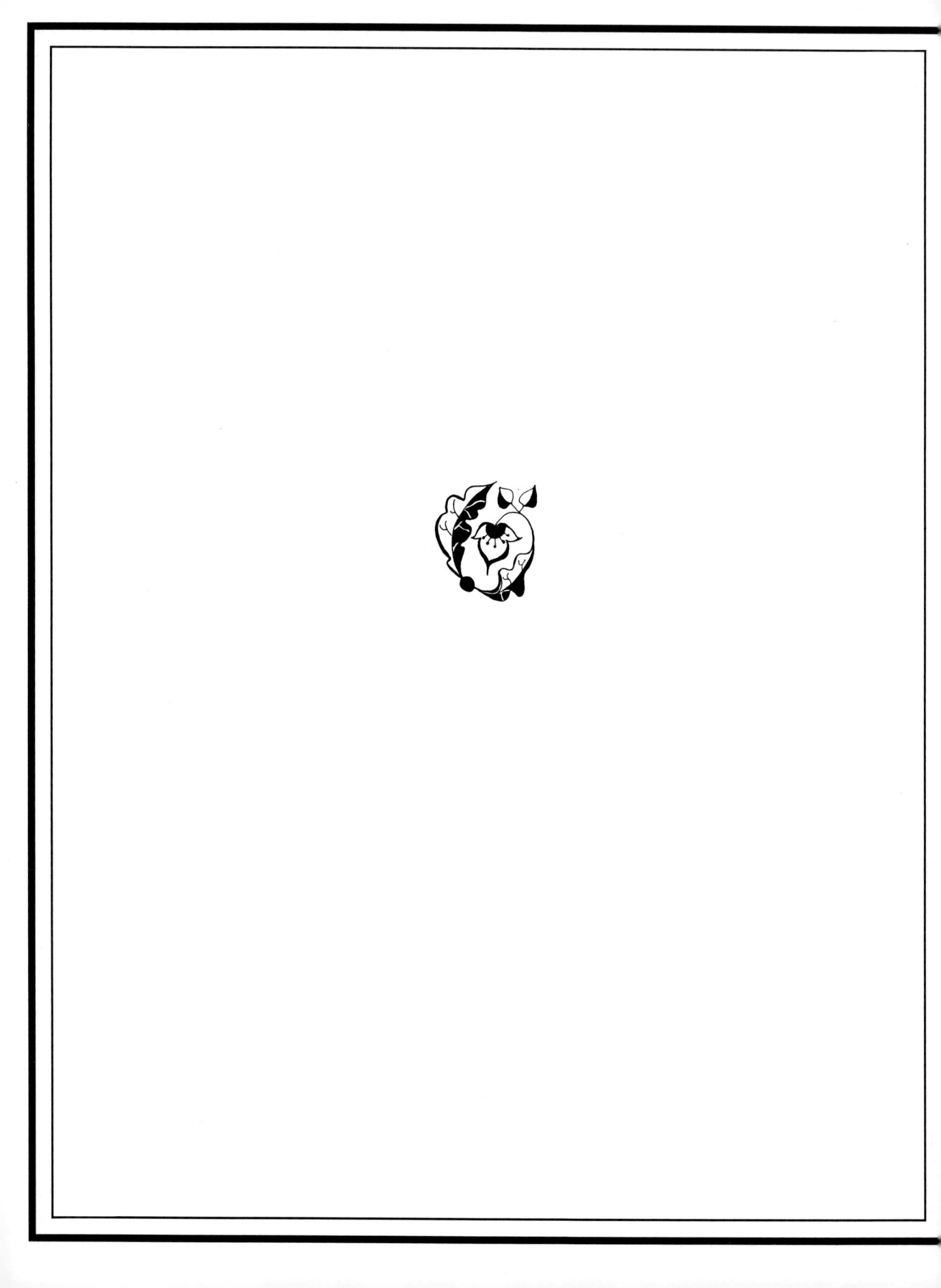

CONTENTS

The Mice of Lardon Hill 9
Pedlar Peg 13
Who Is Out ? 17
Miss Moffat 21
Titus Mouse The Tailor 24
Abdul The Magician 28
Where The Mermaids Sing 35
Percy, The Odd Job Mouse 39
Starlight 43
The Field Mouse And The Fairy 47
Time 51
Story Time 55
Sir Fingal Brutus 59
Madam Phoebe 63
The Winter Queen 67
O Little Town 71
Miss Bustle, Miss Bark And Miss Bell 73
Myrtle Mouse 79
Wedding Bells 83
My Uncle Fred 87
Sir Basil Eye, Detective Mouse 91
The Paradise Tree 95
The Dreamspinner 99
Playtime 103
Where Are You Going ? 107
Winter's Night 111
The Weather Show 115
Candy Cherries 119
The Rocking Horse 123
The Ghost 127

The Hermit Mouse 11
The Apple Brandy Lullaby 15
The Flower Seller 19
The Garden Wall 23
Peggy Plum 26
The Cosy Corner Cafe 33
Summer's Here 37
Friendly Company 41
How Far Away Is Fairyland? 45
The Nicest Place On Earth 49
Echo In The Breeze 53
Where In The World 57
Market Day 61
Fothergill's Second Hand Shop 65
Miss Juniper Mouse 69
Hide And Seek 72
Abigail The Witch Mouse 77
Butterfly 81
The Brigand Mice 85
Thomas Mouse Lost 89
To Play A Double Bass 93
Castles In The Air 97
Petunia Mouse 100
Come With Me 105
The Crossroads 109
Doctor Amos Periwinkle 113
Come To The Barn Dance Tonight 117
The Wishing Stone 121
Blackberries Ripe 125

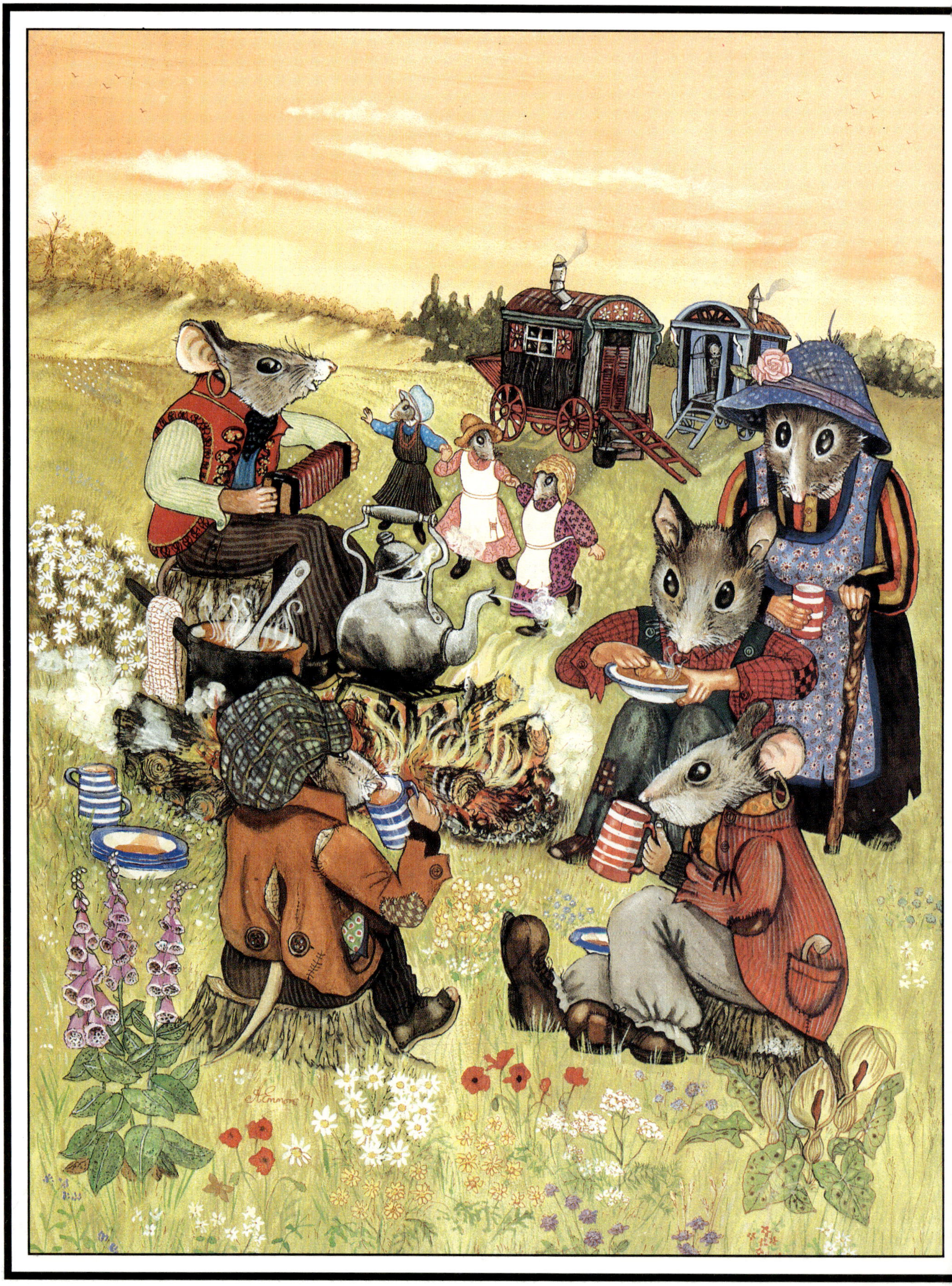

THE MICE OF LARDON HILL

I watched them come and see them still,
The Gypsy Mice of Lardon Hill.
Their Caravans were Weather Worn,
Their shabby clothes were patched and torn.
Their pots and pans were black as soot,
As were their Children, Head to Foot.

I watched them gather Kindling Wood
And lay a fire to cook their food.
The flames blazed high to boil their Stew
And toast their Bread and warm their Brew.
And as they ate, Brave tales they told
Of places seen and Times of Old.

The light grew dim, the air turned chill
And Night time fell on Lardon Hill.
The Gypsy Mice to bed did creep,
Warm and drowsy, soon to sleep.
And then my Eyes grew heavy too,
And when I woke the Day was new.

The Sunlight fell upon the Hill
And Skylarks sang. I hear them still.
But all the Caravans had gone.
The Gypsy Mice had travelled on.
From dying embers smoke curled high
Then disappeared before my Eye.

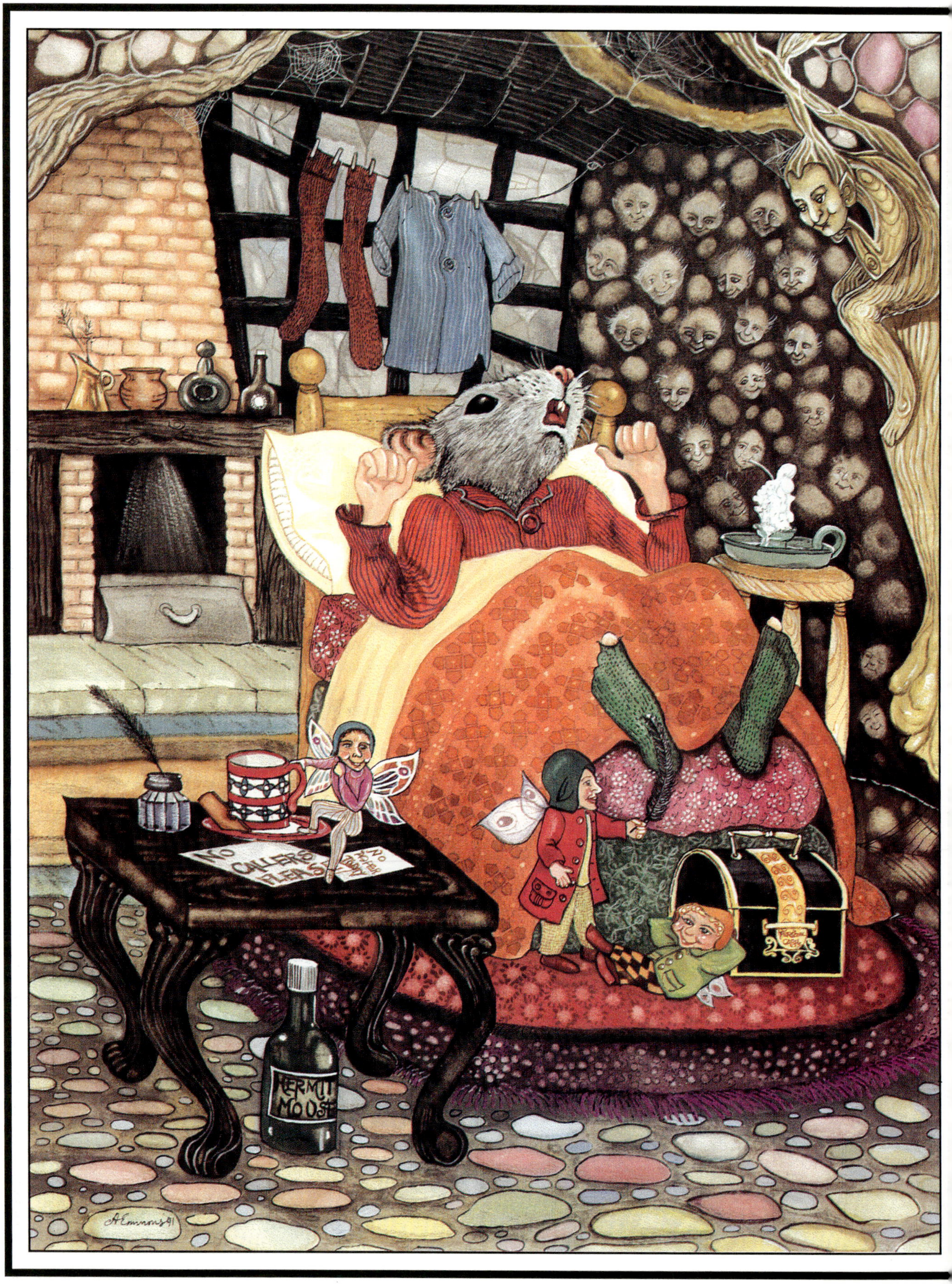
NO
CALLERS
HERMIT

THE HERMIT MOUSE

Deep in a long lost hole in the World
Where Daylight never dawns
The Hermit Mouse is waking up,
He scratches, blinks and yawns.

He asks Himself what kind of day
It is and then replies
That since the hole is rather dark
It seems dull to his Eyes.
And since the air seems rather damp
There must be mist about.
So just as always he decides
It's not worth going out.
He pulls his worn old blanket round,
It is his closest friend,
Then back to sleep he drifts once more
To Darkness without end.

12

PEDLAR PEG

Here she comes, down our Street,
With her big black bonnet and worn out feet.
Selling her wares from an old cloth pack
That she carries round on her hunched up back.
Beads and thimbles, bobbins and bows,
Where she comes from no one knows.

She knocks on doors and gives her cry,
"Come look and feel and smell and try.
Lavender, Ladies, From my tray,
That's the Luck you'll buy today!"
Boot black, brushes, snuff for your nose.
Where she goes to no one knows.

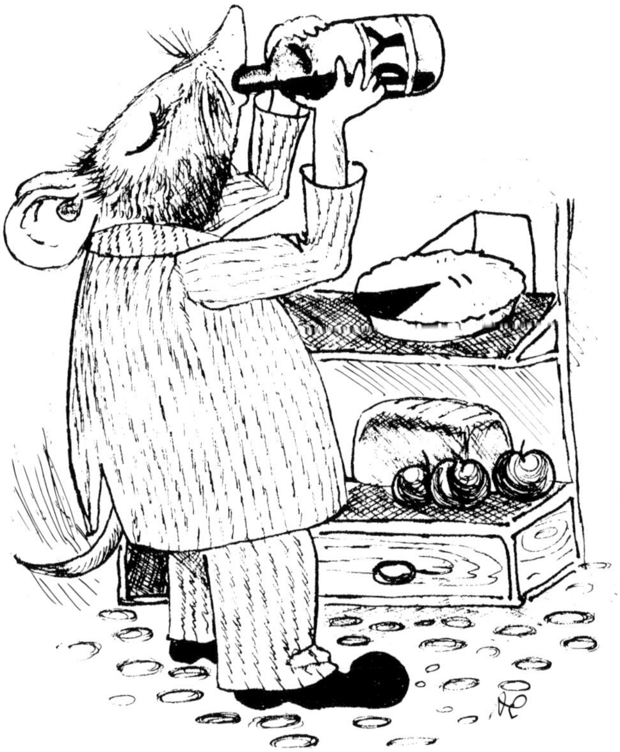

THE APPLE BRANDY LULLABY

Sing a song of Sleeping Mice
Snuggled up in bed.
Three have their feet
Where another has his Head.
Two read by Candlelight,
Another drinks his tea
And puts his cup and Saucer
Where his brother Mouse should be.
One counts the stars
That through the Window Shine,
And wonders why there's eight in bed
When there should be Nine.

When all these Mice are fast asleep
And snoring loud and Clear,
Another Mouse creeps into bed
Beside his Brothers Dear.
He'd visited the Pantry
To eat a Cottage Pie
Then drank the Apple Brandy
And sang their Lullaby.

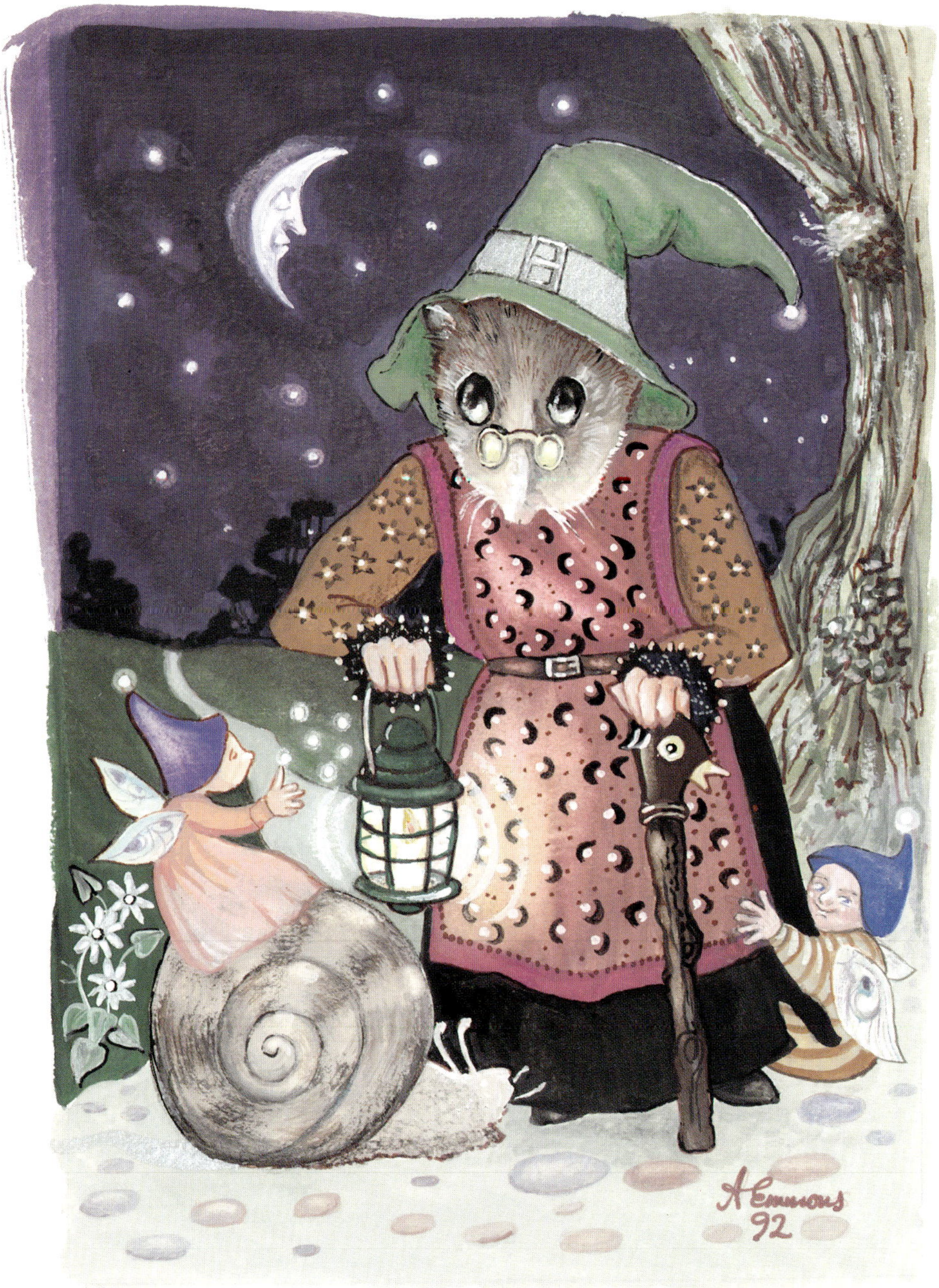
A Emmons
92

WHO IS OUT?

Who is out this Starry Night
Who besides the Moon?
Snails that crawl,
Fairies feint
And Night owls all.

Gypsies, tramps and those who have
No place to rest their head
Must travel on
By candle light
While we're asleep in bed.

18

THE FLOWER SELLER

Who will buy my posies gay
Made from blossoms picked today?
Roses red and Cornflowers blue,
Lilies fresh as morning dew.
Who would see their beauty shine
Smell their perfume sweet as wine?

Violets shy, poppies bold,
Jasmine with its sprigs of gold.
Hollyhocks and Lupins tall,
Saxifrage with flowers so small.
On this grey and foggy day
Buy my blooms to cheer your way!

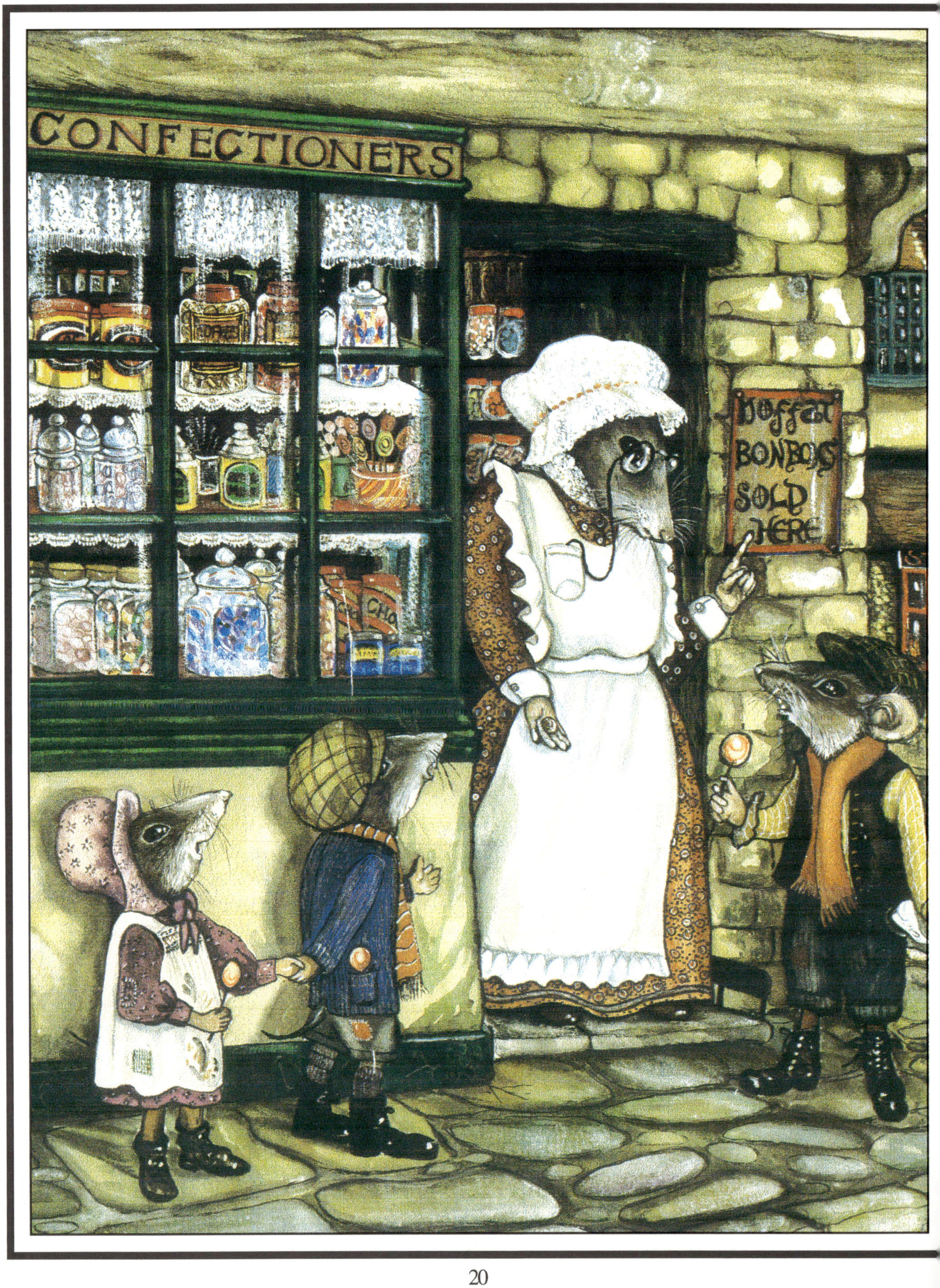
CONFECTIONERS
Moffat
BONBONS
SOLD
HERE

MISS MOFFAT

Miss Moffat keeps the sweet shop on the corner
And it's full of lovely things inside.
There are rows of jars full to the brim with candies
On the polished shelves so deep and wide.
There are licorice twirls, and lemon whirls,
And lollipops of yellow, red and green.
There are chocolate delights and tasty toffee bites
And the biggest bonbons ever seen.

Now Miss Moffat is a crosspatch with a sharp tongue,
And some children have to watch their P's and Q's
When they step into her shop with pocket money
For their bubblegum and little penny chews.
For they are not those gentlemen of breeding
Who purchase gift wrapped boxes for their wives,
They're just the poorest village children
Who've rarely tasted chocolate in their lives.

They gaze up at Miss Moffat's tasty window
And count the pennies they have saved to spend
And sometimes if they're short they'll add a button
Taken from a coat too worn to mend.
For Miss Moffat is so busy watching fingers,
And weighing things exactly to the ounce,
That just maybe she'll be slow to see,
And just as slow to pounce.

Just Maybe!

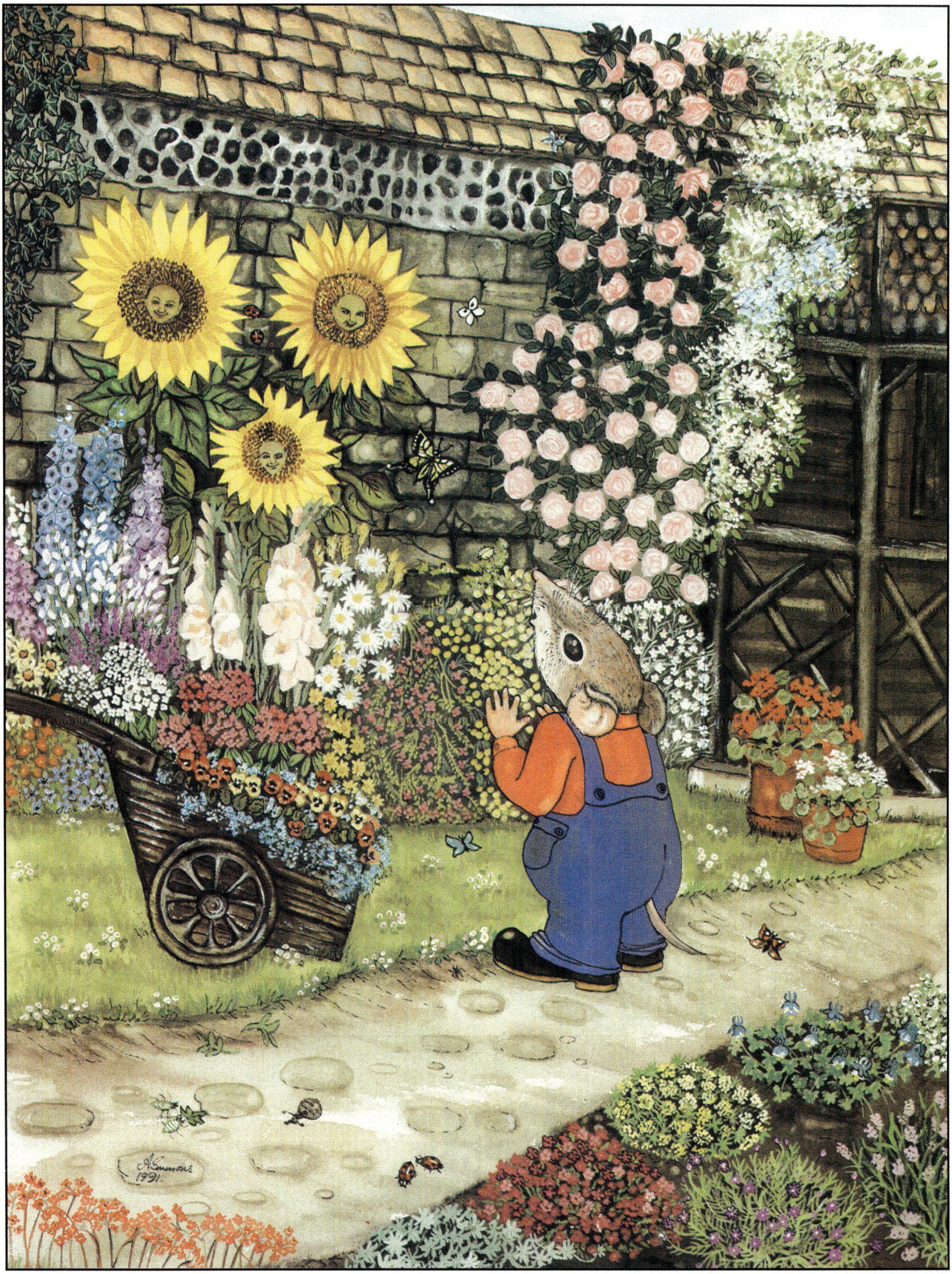
A.Emmons
1991.

THE GARDEN WALL

My home is in a Garden
So beautiful to see,
That's filled with merry Bird Song,
And buzz of Honey Bee.

I know each path and where it leads,
And places you can hide,
Cool and dry and shady
To curl and sleep inside.

I know just where the Garden ends,
Beside the Garden Wall,
And just what lies beyond that,
I cannot see at all.

For that is where my World Ends
And all beyond's a Dream.
For what are Valleys, Hills and Fields,
Seas and Lakes and Streams?

It is too high for me to climb,
To see what lies Outside,
And if I saw how grand it was,
Would I be satisfied?

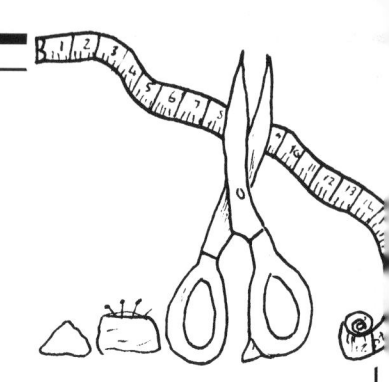

TITUS MOUSE THE TAILOR

Clothes for all occasions,
Made in every size,
With quality Outstanding
Titus Mouse supplies.
His shop is long established,
Respected and Renowned,
He's quite the finest Tailor
For Gentle-Mice around.
His suits are made to measure
And cut with loving Care
From all the finest fabrics
For Customers to wear.

His shop is painted Green and Gold
It's in the Village Square,
With model Mice in sporting pose
Stood in the Window there.
It's always very busy,
And if you want to buy,
You'll not be disappointed
At what may catch your eye.

Silk and Satin Waistcoats
In colours bright and bold
Hang smartly to attention
Waiting to be sold.
Ties and Socks and pairs of gloves
Each have a special Drawer,
And deep beneath the Counter
Lie Handkerchiefs galore.
Hats, the Height of Fashion
Are boxed up on the Floor,
And Overcoats in sombre shades
Stand ready by the door.

A busy Mouse is Titus
Pernickety, Precise,
A striver for Perfection,
A Paragon of Mice.
His shop is open Nine to Five,
And not a Minute more,
So hurry now or you may find
The 'CLOSED' sign on the door.

PEGGY PLUM

Peggy Plum loves housework,
She does it all the time!
You'll never meet a Mouse so Neat
Whose home is quite as fine!

She scrubs the steps on Mondays
And polishes the floors,
Then dusts around the skirtings,
The cupboards and the doors.

On Tuesdays if the Weather's fine
She cleans the Window Panes
But only does the inside bits
If it snows or rains.

She sweeps the yard on Wednesdays
And digs the garden too,
Poking out each little weed
As soon as it comes through.

On Thursdays she goes shopping
But first she checks her store
For jams and Cheese and Pickles
In case she needs some more.

She bakes her bread on Fridays
And wipes her larder out,
Then waters all the pot plants
And cleans the teapot spout.

On Saturdays she scrubs her clothes,
And fills the washing line
With Sheets of palest Satin
And lingerie so fine.

But Sunday is her favourite Day
When friends come round to tea
And stare in admiration
At the best kept home to see.

ABDUL THE MAGICIAN

Abdul the Magician,
The finest in the Land,
Could conjure up great Wonders
With his cunning sleight of hand.
He was a great performer,
The crowds just loved his show,
And watched his tricks with bated breath,
Their faces all aglow.
His act grew so remarkable
That he began to boast
"I can conjure up a Genie,
Or a Goblin, or a Ghost!"

And so the King commanded him
To cast a special spell
And bring to Earth for all to see
The Princess Sunrayelle.
She was the Princess of the sun
Whose Father, in his might,
Breathed flames of Gold upon the Earth
To keep it warm and bright.

As Abdul's greatest act began,
The King and Court all saw
A Giant Urn embossed in Gold
Rise slowly from the floor.
Then Abdul waved his Magic Rod,
A crack of Thunder roared,
And from that urn so dazzling bright
Great golden sovereigns poured.
And then a Flash, a puff of smoke,

The Sun Princess stood there!
A creature bright and beautiful
With gem stones in her hair.
The audience were all amazed
As Abdul took her hand,
And led the Princess gently up
To the King's great Royal Stand.

The King embraced the Princess
And took her to his side,
And told his loyal Citizens
That she would be his bride.
But then the sky went black as pitch,
And a mighty cry of grief
Roared down from Heaven over Earth,
"Where is my Daughter, Thief?
The Princess of the Sun is gone,
My Daughter, my Delight,
Stolen from my side this day
Whilst casting Sunbeams bright.

The sky will stay in Darkness
Until she comes again
No Queen on Earth my child will be
For by my side she'll reign."
The King looked very angry
Yet trembled as he spoke,
"Oh, Sun King Bright I love the night
Your warning is a joke!"
"So be it" cried the Lord of Light
"So be it foolish King,
I'll have you begging on your knees
Before we speak again!"

And so the Earth for many months
In Darkness did remain.
The crops and trees all withered up,
And then the famine came.
The King and Princess Sunrayelle
Were shouted at with scorn,
And hungry folk grew weak and tired
Of waiting for the Dawn.

Now Sunrayelle, she loved the King,
She loved her father too,
And so she sought the Great Abdul
To tell her what to do.
He thought a while then sadly smiled,
And gently took her hand,
"What I must do will break your heart,
But try to understand.
I will return you to the Sun
The very way you came,
Two hearts will break, two lovers part,
But light will come again."

And so it was as Abdul said,
And Sunrayelle returned,
And once again the Sun King shone
On land that he had spurned.
But heavy raindrops blotted out
The Sunbeams as they fell,
As tears of anguish and despair
Were shed by Sunrayelle.
Her Father could not comfort her,
He could not ease her pain,
And so decided she must go
Back to her love again.
He made a splendid chariot,
"A farewell gift" said he,
"You love the King on Earth much more
Than you can now love me".
And so it was that Sunrayelle
Returned to Earth below,
And from afar The Sun shone out
His warm but lonely glow.

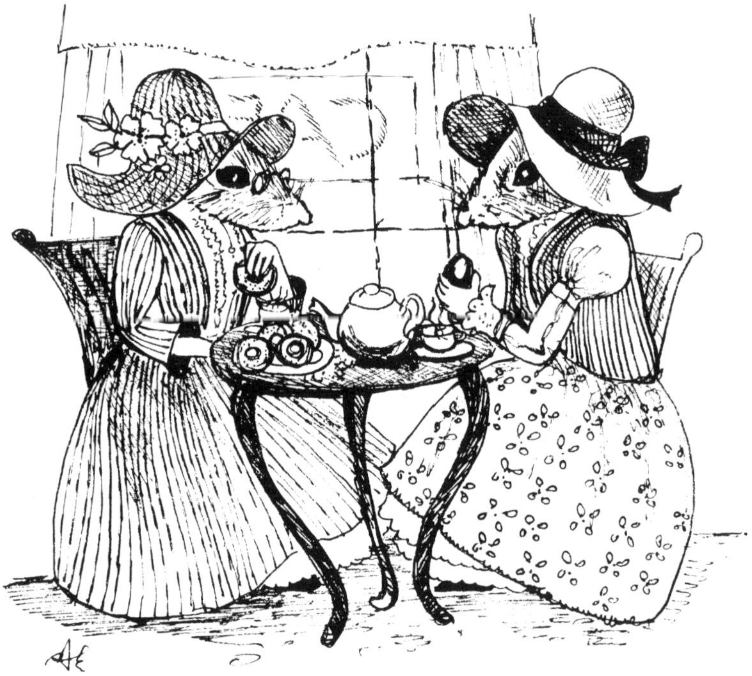

THE COSY CORNER CAFE

If you've a few moments to spare
I'd love to take you there,
To sample muffins freshly baked
And other tasty fare.
The kettle singing all day long
Will welcome you with cheerful song.
The blazing fire will beg you stay
Indoors from a damp and sunless day.

If you've a sweet tooth you'll agree
This is the place to be.
With pastries, cream buns, apple pies
And such delicious tea.
The treacle tart is quite divine
Served hot with custard, mighty fine!
And no one minds how long you stay
As long as when you leave you pay!

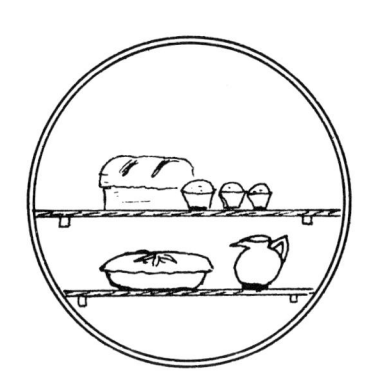

34

WHERE THE MERMAIDS SING

Have you ever sailed where the Mermaids Sing
By a turquoise blue lagoon
Or seen the Silver Fishes jump
To the lonely Crescent Moon?
Waters calm and waters deep,
Steady as we go!
We'll ride the salty seas again
You Landlubbers below!

Now Seven Sailors bold are we
All for adventure bound.
We've heard of wondrous stories told
Of sunken treasure found,
Of sirens calling Mice and Men
Down to their deaths below,
Of seas that toss and churn and boil
On which the wild winds blow.

So haul away the anchor boys,
We're sailing on the tide,
And say farewell to your fair friend
Who's standing by your side.
The World is calling us to see
The Wonders she's in store.
Beyond the grey Horizon
You will never see us more.

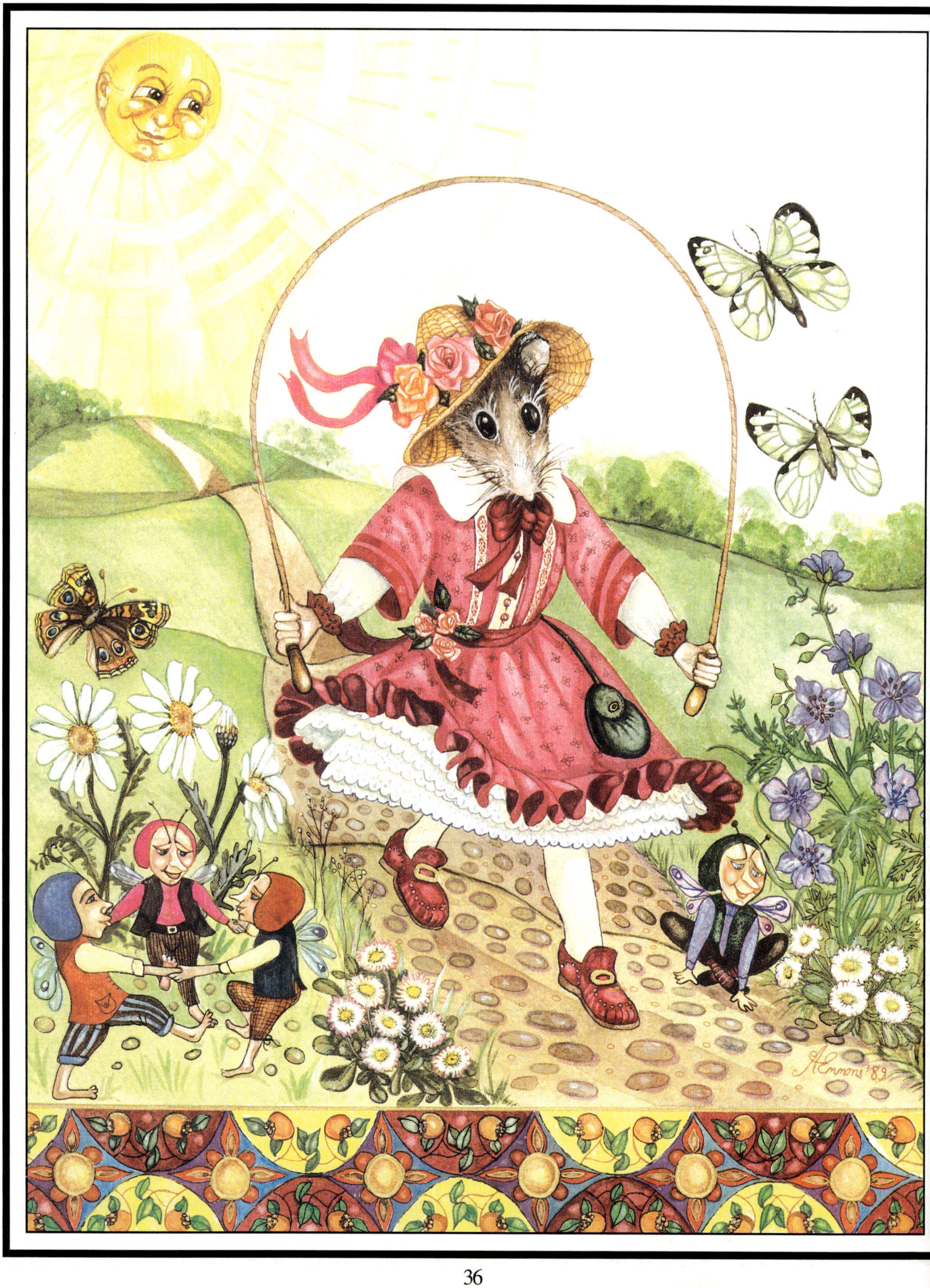

SUMMER'S HERE

Skip for joy
Now Summer's here
And all the fields are green.
Sing with the lark
High in the sky
And dance by
The laughing stream.

Gentle winds blow
Where they will
Through the meadows
And o'er the hill.
Let them waft you
While they may
On your carefree
Merry way.

For all too soon
The time will come
When Summer reigns no more
Then leaves so fragile
Wither, die,
And fall 'neath
The forest floor.

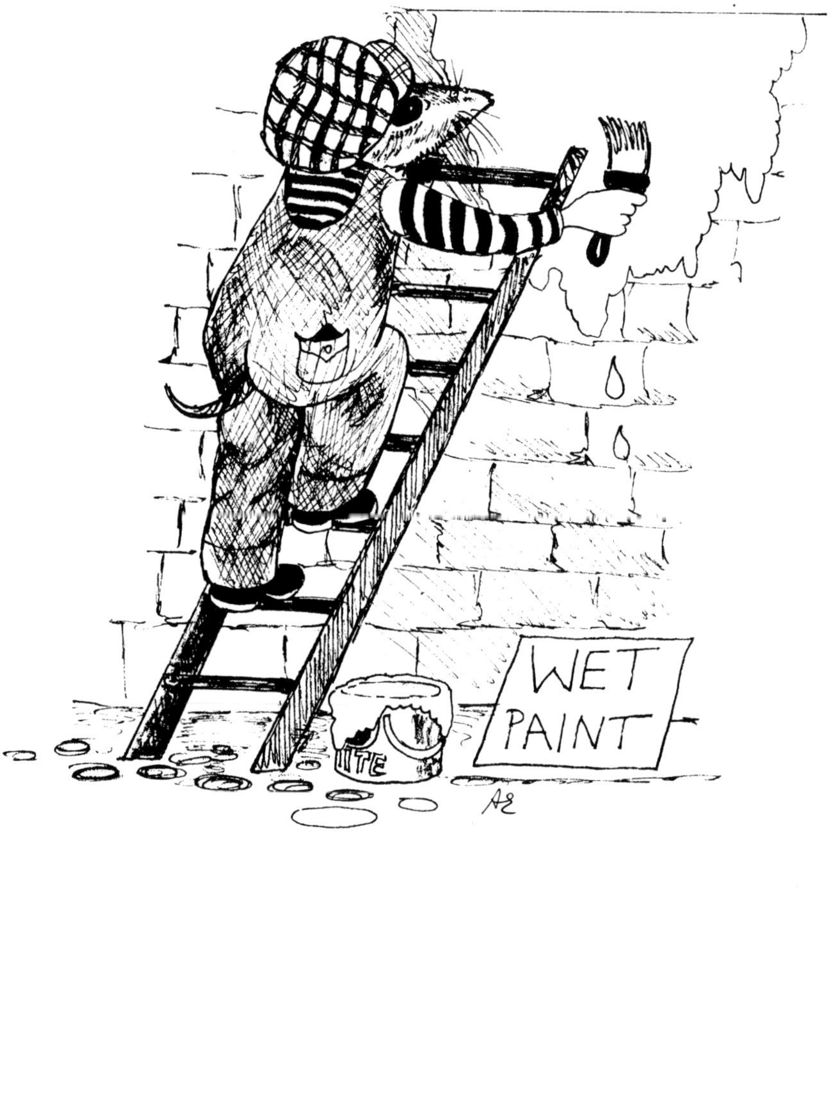
WET
PAINT

PERCY, THE ODD JOB MOUSE

Any Odd Jobs to do today?
Fences to fix or tiles to lay?
Walls to paint, Windows to mend,
Pipes to clean out round the bend?

Percy Mouse will do the Work,
He's never been a one to shirk.
The most unpleasant undertaking
To him is money in the making.

He'll mend your broken chairs and stools,
Fit new bits on damaged tools,
Sharpen knives and make them shine,
Fix your broken washing line.

When something seems beyond repair
Just send for Percy, he'll be there.
"I'll have a look at that", he'll say
And it'll be good as new next day.

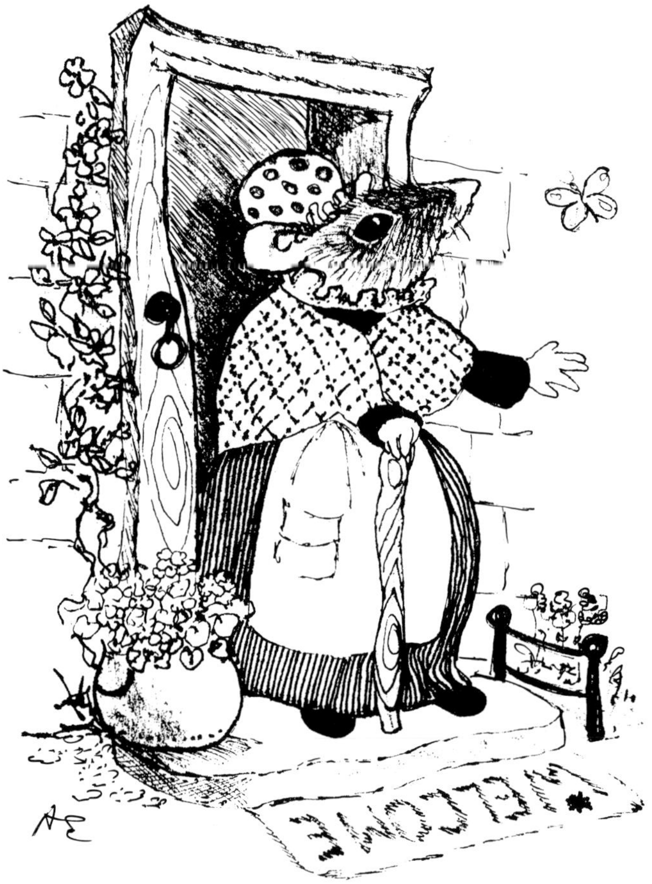
WELCOME

FRIENDLY COMPANY

No one has passed this way
For many a weary day.
So come in for a while
And warm me with your Smile.
Tell me of the World
Beyond my own closed door
And tell me News of Folk
Who used to call before.
Too old to reach the outside
Which never reaches me,
I long for just a little taste
Of Friendly Company.

42

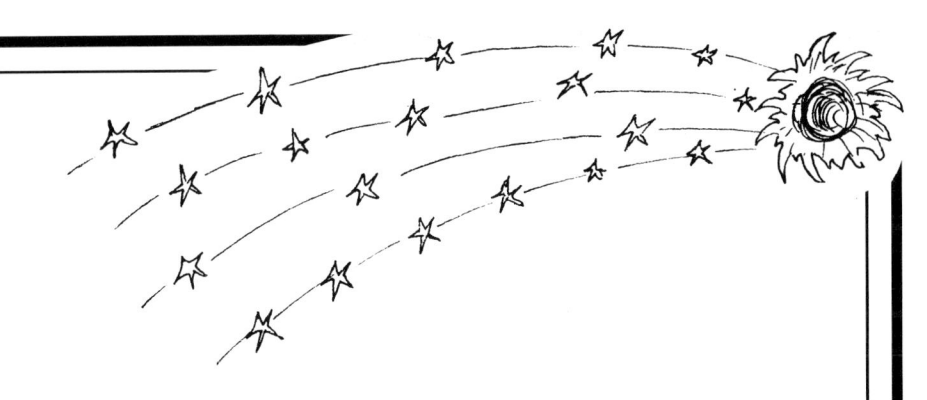

STARLIGHT

How far do you travel Starlight,
Beyond the Milky Way,
Through Space as black as Caverns Deep
Beyond the reach of day?
May I travel with you,
A million miles or more,
Out of reach of Time and Place
Strange new Worlds to explore?

Will I see great Monsters
On Planets floating by,
Who call out in their loneliness
A distant soundless cry?
Will I spend a lifetime
Seeking out the Star
That somewhere back in History
Made you what you are?

44

HOW FAR AWAY IS FAIRY LAND?

How far away is Fairy Land?
Shall I ever know
Which hidden footpath I must take
And which way I must go?
Shall I travel there in style
On Stallion black as Night,
A Fairy Princess for a day
In gown so rich and bright?
Shall I find the toadstools
Where little Elf Folk dwell,
And will I see real Goblins
Living down a well?
I'd visit darkest forests
Where Sprites and Witches go
And follow magic Rivers
To Lands of Mist and Snow.
I'd take the footpath all the way
To Castles by the Sea,
With Turrets high and Cellars deep
And doors without a Key.
And when my journey's over
How happy I shall be
To think a special place is there
Beyond Reality.

46

THE FIELD MOUSE AND THE FAIRY

One night in the middle of Winter
The Forest lay fast asleep.
The stars twinkled down from the heavens,
The snow lay soft and deep.
All the wild creatures were sleeping
Deep in their dark little holes,
The foxes, the rabbits and squirrels,
The badgers and weasels and moles.
But one little creature was restless,
A waif of a field mouse was he
Lying awake and all alone
And hungry as can be.
He set out to hunt for some berries
Under the frosty night sky,
But the snow was drifting, the wind was cold,
And he began to cry.

Now under the snow lived a fairy,
Who only came out in the Spring.
She woke up from her dreaming
When a tear fell on her wing.
The tear was warm
And so she thought
That Spring had come again,
She shook the snowdrops from her hair
And peered up from her den.
She saw the poor little field mouse,
All alone in the snow.
She knew that he was hungry,
Her magic told her so.
She waved her wand
And on the snow
Ripe nuts and berries fell.
The little field mouse ate and ate
Until he felt quite well.

He never again saw the fairy,
But somehow from then on
He knew he had a friend somewhere.
His loneliness was gone.

THE NICEST PLACE ON EARTH

I don't know where I live,
I couldn't show you where
In the World I am;
But I'll take you there!

I've never seen a Map
Of the Field of Corn
With its Hedgerows Deep
Where I was born.

But I know my Home
Is deep beneath the Ground
In a cosy little Hole
That I once found.

Sheltered from the Weather,
Safe as Safe can be,
It's the Nicest Place
On Earth for Me!

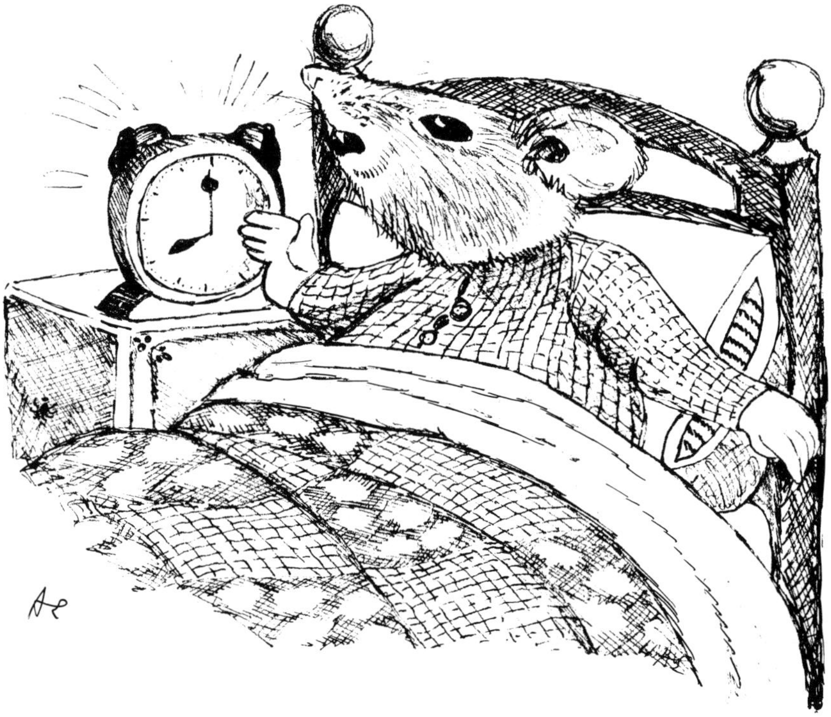

TIME

Playtime, Teatime,
Time for Bed.
Time to wake up
Sleepy Head!
The hours march by,
All day Long,
Tick-Tock, Tick-Tock,
Tick-Tock, GONE!

Happy Moments
Won't you Stay?
Don't rush wildly
On your way,
When you disappear
Forever,
May that be the END
Of NEVER.

52

ECHO IN THE BREEZE

Come Fairy Mice
And gather round
To hear our music play.
The night is warm,
The stars are bright,
And moonbeams light your way.
Our songs will make you
Laugh and cry
And tap your feet and dance,
With pretty-ditty
Roundelay
And ballads of Romance.

Your Time is fleeting
As the Night
And soon will come the Day
When Shadow Folk
The likes of us
Must surely fade away.
So hear our Music
Boldly shake
The leaves of sleeping Trees
For by and by
It drifts away
An echo in the Breeze.

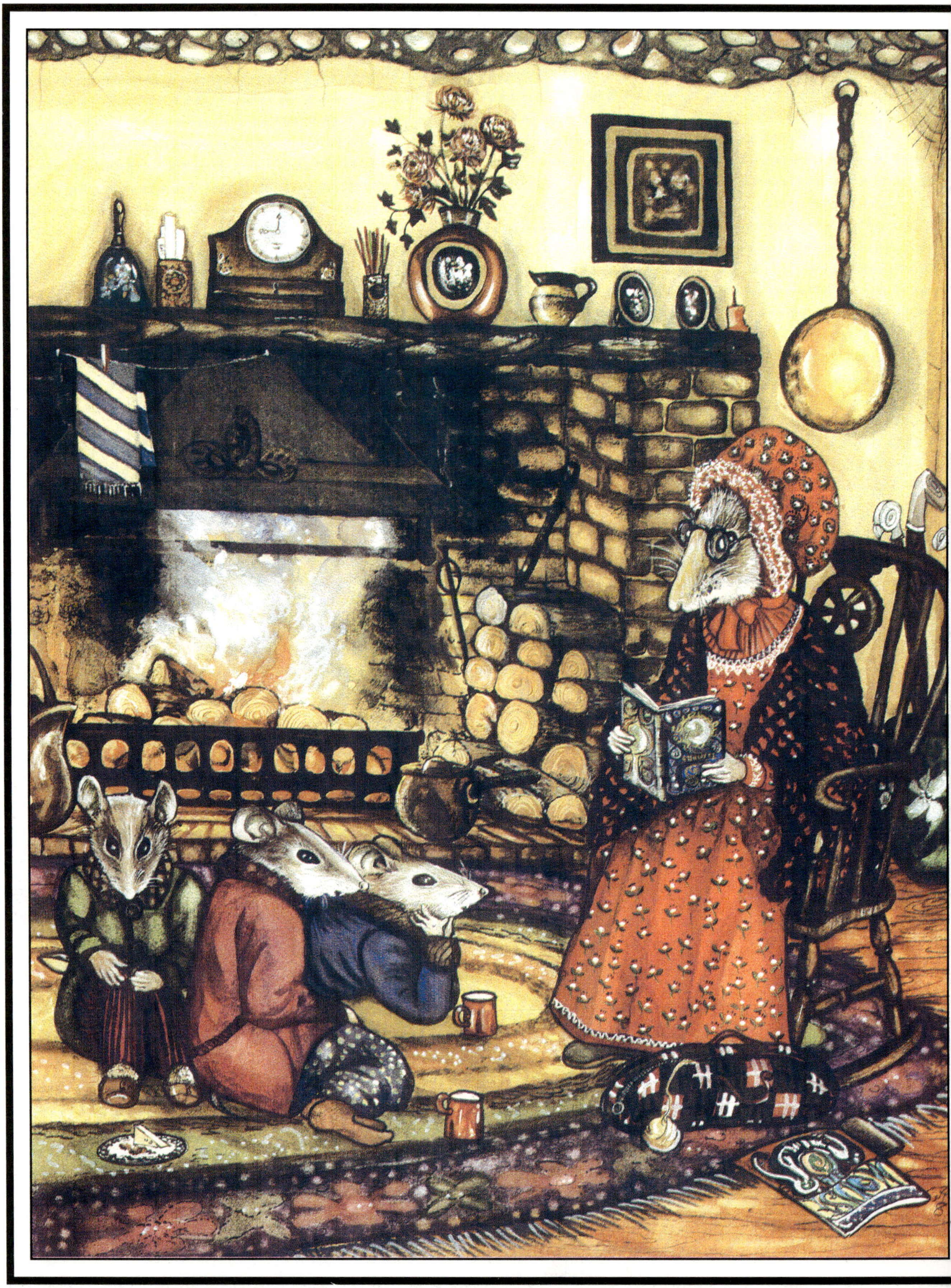

STORY TIME

Tell us a story Grandma
Before we go to bed.
The one about the White Knight
Who strikes the Dragon dead.
The one about the Princess
Who cannot sleep at all.
The one about the Beanstalk
That grows so big and tall.
We're happy just to listen
Though we've heard them all before.
And if you finish that book
We can find you many more.

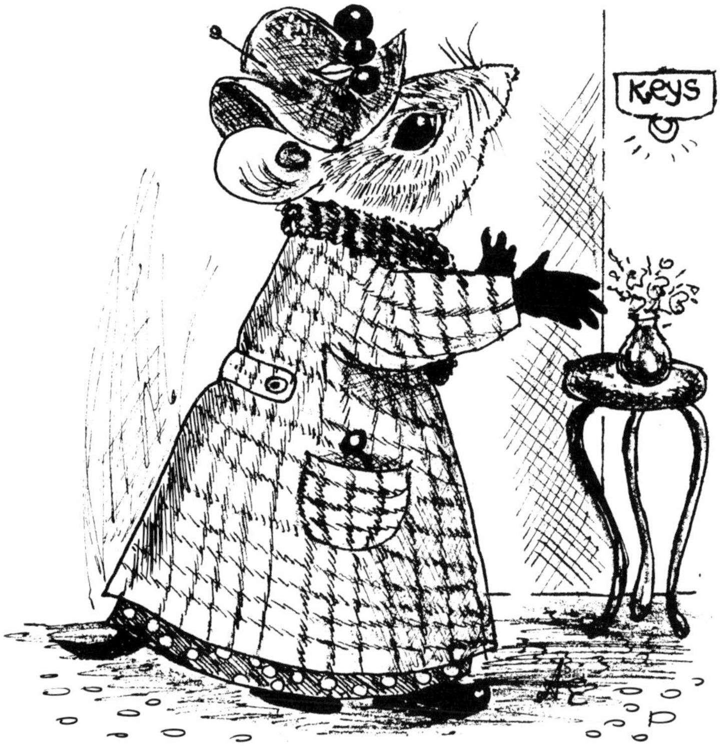
Keys

WHERE IN THE WORLD

Where in the world did I put my key?
It's gone somewhere that I can't see.
It's not on the shelf and not in the drawer,
Nor anywhere I've looked before.
I can't lock the door, so I can't go out,
In case there are thieves lurking about.
Besides, it's foggy, cold and wet,
And old Hannah Mouse may well forget
That she invited me for tea.
I should be there by ten to three!
And I've got Muffins fresh to eat
To take her for a special Treat!
They'll taste delicious spread with Honey,
And Butter warmed and thick and runny.
I may as well just eat them here,
They're really quite sensational Dear!
And look, my key was in my Hat!
Upon the Table! Fancy that!
I may as well go out to Tea
For Hannah Mouse needs Company!
She won't mind if I'm rather late,
She'll keep her Tarts out on the plate.
I'll take a cake I've baked instead,
I know she's fond of Gingerbread.
Her stomach is too delicate
To take fresh Muffins served so late.
It's for the best, I'm sure of that!
I'd go right now...........But where's my Hat?

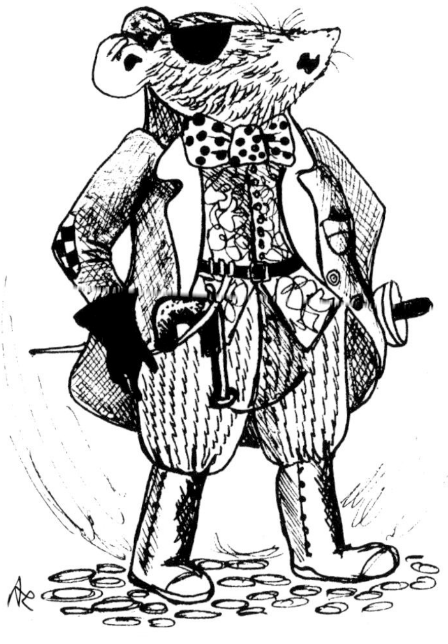

SIR FINGAL BRUTUS

There is a Mouse whose name
Is whispered far and wide.
He's called Sir Fingal Brutus
And his home is Lardon Ride.

Sir Fingal is a Villain,
A Mouse who loves a fight,
Whose blunderbuss is loaded,
Ready day and night.

He stalks his woods for trespassers
And greets them with his gun
Then roars with raucous laughter
When they turn and run.

He terrorises Lady Mice
Who think he's really Mad
For his language is appalling
And his manners just as bad.

Some say he has a fortune
Safely locked away
And hopefully he'll join it
One not too distant day!

60

MARKET DAY

Come and buy! Come and buy!
Come and hear the Market Cry.

Pears and apples, Cherries Ripe,
Cheeses, hams and butcher's tripe.
Jellied eels and speckled eggs,
Pickles, spices, fresh nutmegs.

Studs and buttons, reels of thread,
Laces white and ribbons red.
Pins and needles, darning wool,
Empty packets, bobbins full.

Pots and pans, bowls and plates,
Painted brightly, stacked in eights.
Vases tall and teapots fat,
Spoons and forks and things like that.

Scrubbing brushes, Bric-a-brac,
Sponges heaped up in a sack,
Teatowels, floorcloths, dusters gay,
Brighten up our Market Day.

Gypsy Phoebe
Fortunes Told

MADAM PHOEBE

Madam Phoebe the Fortune Teller
Has a crystal ball down in her cellar.
In the dark it really glows
As on it Phoebe gently blows,
And deep inside strange patterns form
All misty as an Autumn dawn,
And nobody can clearly see
What these ghostly shapes may be.

But Phoebe stares into the ball,
And clearly she can see it all,
As slowly in a frightening way
She rolls her eyes and starts to say
What path your life can safely take
To spare you sorrow and heartache,
And disappointment, grief and woe,
Who is your friend and who your foe.

Now Phoebe studies Palmistry
And Heavenly Astrology.
She knows the birthsigns and the Stars
The influence of Moon and Mars.
She knows the head line and the heart,
And practises such cunning art.
But most of all she dotes on money,
And thinks her clients rather funny.
For a glimpse of the future they pay their fee
And Phoebe's eyes light up with glee.

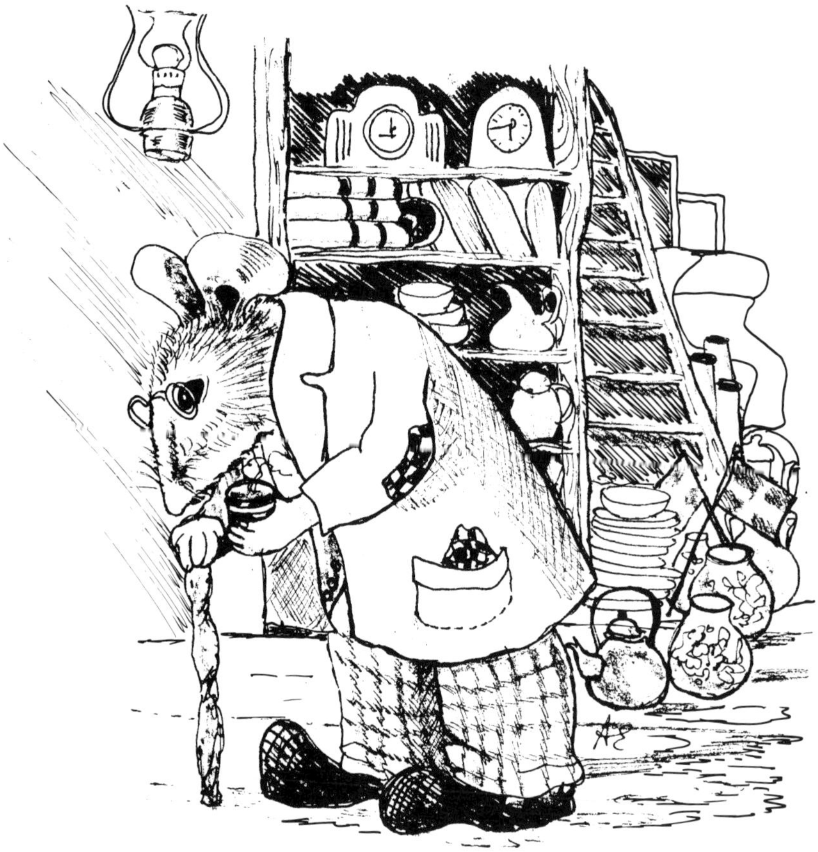

FOTHERGILL'S SECOND HAND SHOP

A squeaking hinge, a Musty smell.
The jangle of an old door-bell.
A well stocked shop where gaslight falls
On gloomy pictures on the walls.
And rows of old decaying books
Lie stacked up high where no one looks
To see the thoughts recorded there,
In finest style with greatest care.
And dying clocks which tick and chime
And strike another hour and time,
Lie side by side upon the floor
With china plates and pots galore.
Where long awaiting small repairs
Stand seven idle old armchairs.
And children's toys lie row on row
Abandoned many years ago.

A creaking door, shuffling feet.
No customers today to greet
Old Fothergill who lives upstairs,
The vendor of these ancient wares.
He glances round as sunlight falls
With shadows dancing round the walls,
And dust twirls idly in the air,
Then sits down in his easy chair,
And waits to see just who may call
To take a look and buy it all.

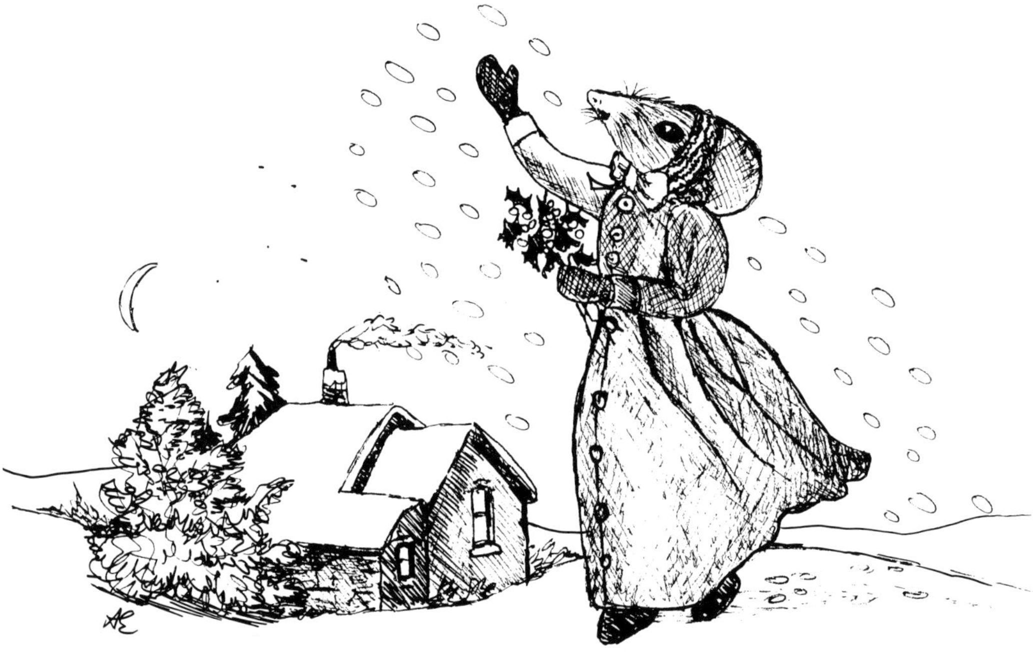

THE WINTER QUEEN

Greet the Winter Queen
As she rides by
In a flurry of Snow
Through the Gloomy Sky.

Greet the Holly
With berries bright
And the Mistletoe
With fruits of White.

Greet the Warmth
Of the fire at Night
And the welcome Glow
Of Candlelight.

Greet Jack Frost
Painting his way
With a palette of
Silvers, blues and Grey.

Greet the Snowdrops
Joyfully
For Heralding Spring
In Dark February.

68

MISS JUNIPER MOUSE

Miss Juniper Mouse has a very cosy house
At the end of Larch Tree Lane
She looks very neat with her mob-cap on
But she really is quite plain.
She works all day by her blazing fire
Sewing things to order
Like dresses, skirts and tablecloths
With plain and fancy border.
She spins and weaves and stitches,
Embroiders and makes lace,
She turns up hems so perfectly
There's no seam out of place.
Miss Juniper is so busy she rarely stops for tea,
She sometimes takes her mid-day meal
As late as half past three.

Now Titus Mouse the tailor
Once asked her for her hand
In Holy Matrimony
But she made him understand
That she had no time for romance
And had no wish to wed.
She preferred her pins and needles
And would rather sew instead.
Miss Juniper Mouse has a very cosy home
At the end of Larch Tree Lane.
Some say she's rather lonely,
Though she never does complain.
Her spinning wheel keeps whirring
From dawn to dusk and on
Her needle sews on through the years
'Till all her thread is gone.

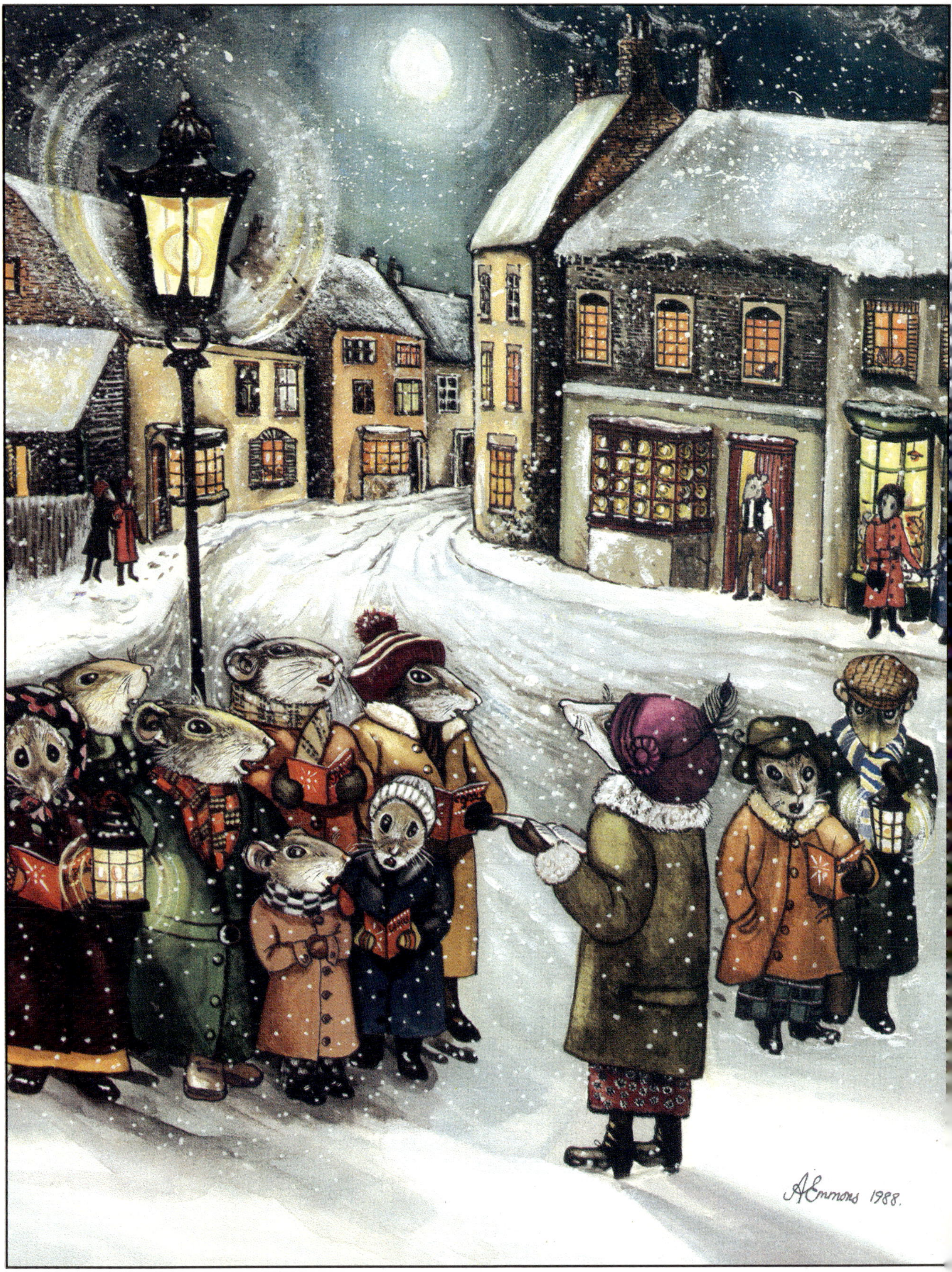
A Emmons 1988.

O LITTLE TOWN

O little town we sing to you
Our carols of great joy.
Beneath the lamp our feet we stamp
And sing of Mary's boy.
For all God's creatures love him,
However great or small,
The weasel, rat, the mouse and cat,
He cares for each and all.

Our hands are cold but hearts are warm
And love will show the way,
So gather round and give your praise
For soon it's Christmas Day.
And though the snow falls all around
And frozen is the moon,
Our lanterns bright will give us light
So hear our happy tune.

HIDE AND SEEK

Let us play at Hide and Seek
Within the Woodland Tall.
Close your eyes and count to ten
Then "Coming!" you may call.

And we will run and vanish
Among a thousand trees,
Lie hidden, still and silent,
And pray we do not sneeze.

Then you will go a hunting
Catch us if you can!
We knew that we could disappear
Before the game began!

MISS BUSTLE, MISS BARK AND MISS BELL

Miss Bustle, Miss Bark and Miss Bell
Are all teachers
(I'm sure you can tell!)
And they meet once a week
For their afternoon tea
(Which looks very tasty,
I'm sure you'll agree).
They talk about reading and writing and maths,
And trips with their pupils along to the baths.
They talk about pupils who cannot behave,
(And here their expressions are frightfully grave).

Miss Bustle has trouble with young Jimmy Brown
Who will not sit up straight and will not sit down.
He looks out the window and looks out the door,
And says that Miss Bustle is rather a bore.

Miss Bark has her 'problems', she shouts at them all
With a high pitched shriek or a raucous bawl.
But we know her bark is much worse than her bite,
And she ticks sums whether they're wrong or right.

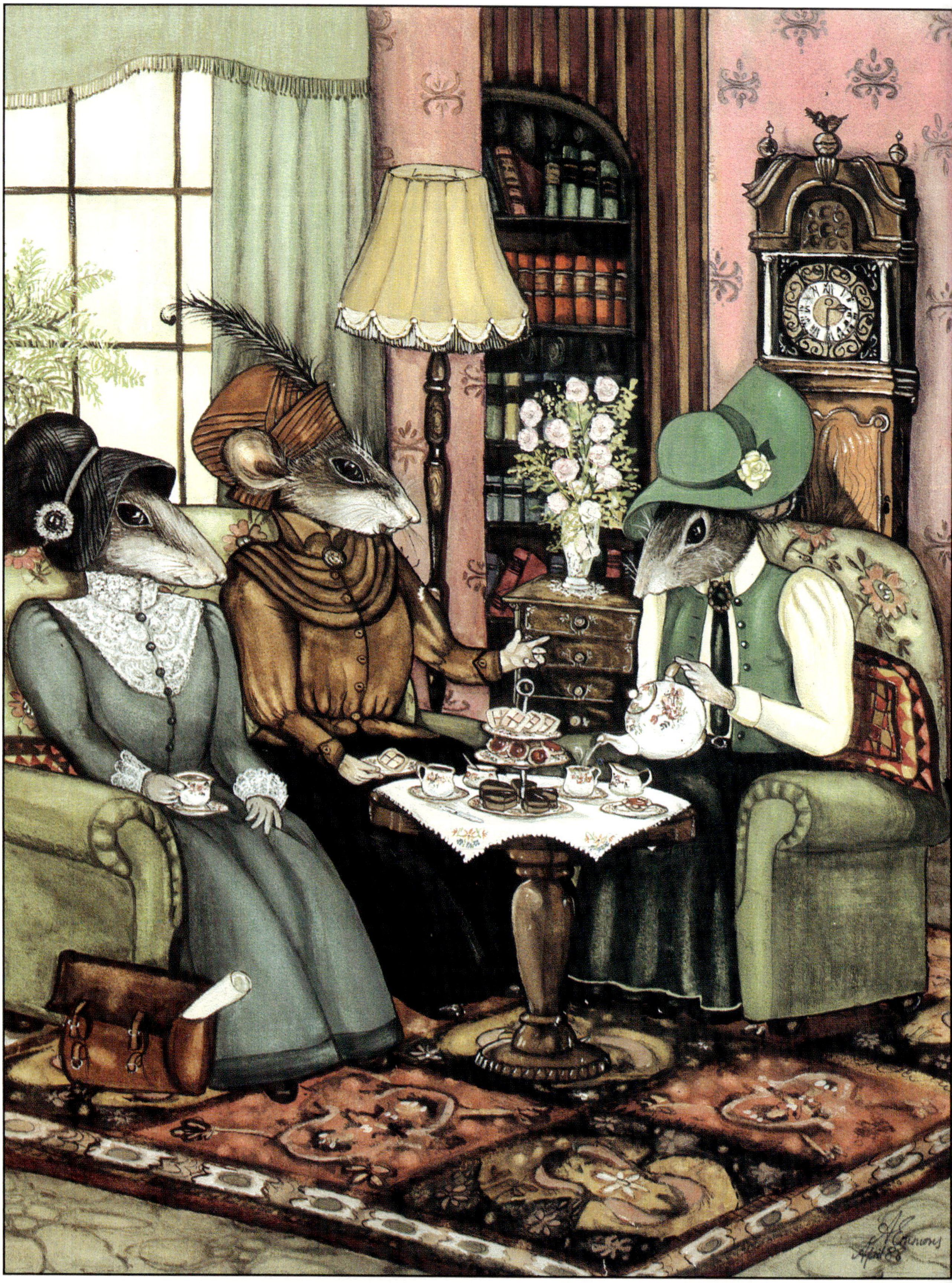

Miss Bell teaches music, (I'm sure you will note),
And she speaks with a melody deep in her throat.
She plays the piano, the flute and the harp,
And sings like a skylark, shrill in 'F' sharp.

Miss Bustle, Miss Bark and Miss Bell
Are old spinsters
(I'm sure you can tell).
And soon they won't meet
For their afternoon tea
That's served precisely
At half past three,
To chatter together and aim to agree
On the finer points of school policy.
And the best ways of teaching the youth of today
Will all be forgotten and filed away.

76

ABIGAIL THE WITCH MOUSE

Abigail, the Witch Mouse
Lives in a quaint house
Underneath an ancient oak.
She sells cures and potions
And magical lotions
To all sorts of curious folk.

Her door is always open wide,
Her wares are stored up high,
Their sweet smell sure to lure you in
To sample and to buy.

There's catmint juice
To calm your cold
And mint to soothe your nerves,
And when you can't get off to sleep
It's lemon balm she serves.
Her lavender and camomile
Are oils so rich and sweet,
Her rose-hip tea with honey served
Is something of a treat!

Though Abigail lives all alone
Her friends are everywhere.
She chatters to them endlessly
When she has time to spare.
They are the plants and insects small
Whose ways she studies well,
Her love and care have captured them
Just like a magic spell!

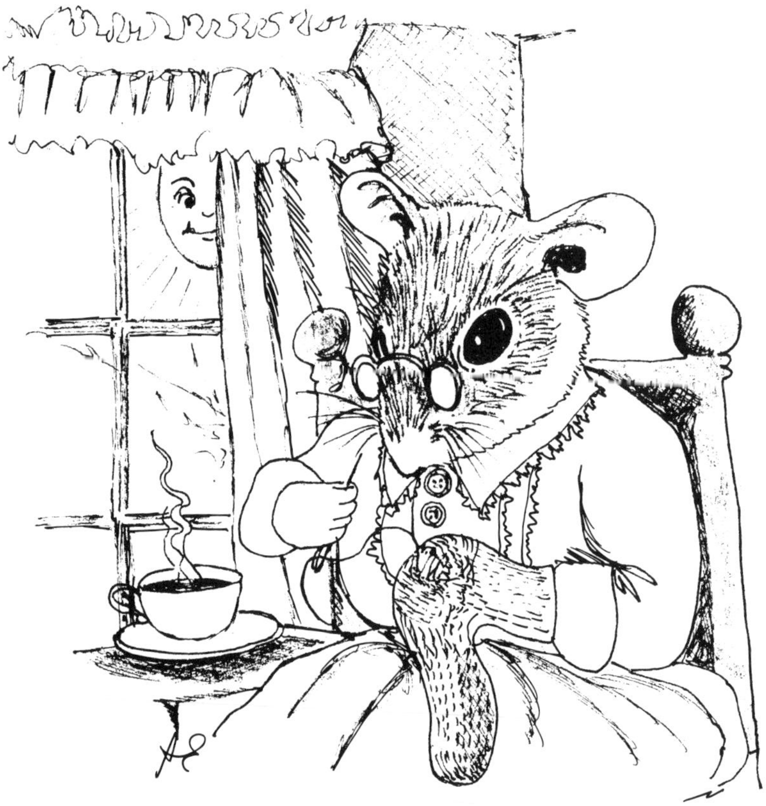

MYRTLE MOUSE

Myrtle Mouse is Old and Wise
And sees the World through twinkling Eyes
That mirror memories of Old,
And sparkle as they still behold
The fleeting Moments passing by
As transient as the Butterfly.

She needs no clock upon the wall
To see the pattern of it all,
To see the smallest Flower unfold
And Blossoms all too soon grow old.
To see the Sun set once again
To hear the beating of the Rain.

She lives beside a tumbling stream
In a little hut that's red and green.
She sews and patches, darns and mends
And does repairs on odds and ends,
And as she works each busy day
She sings the happy hours away.

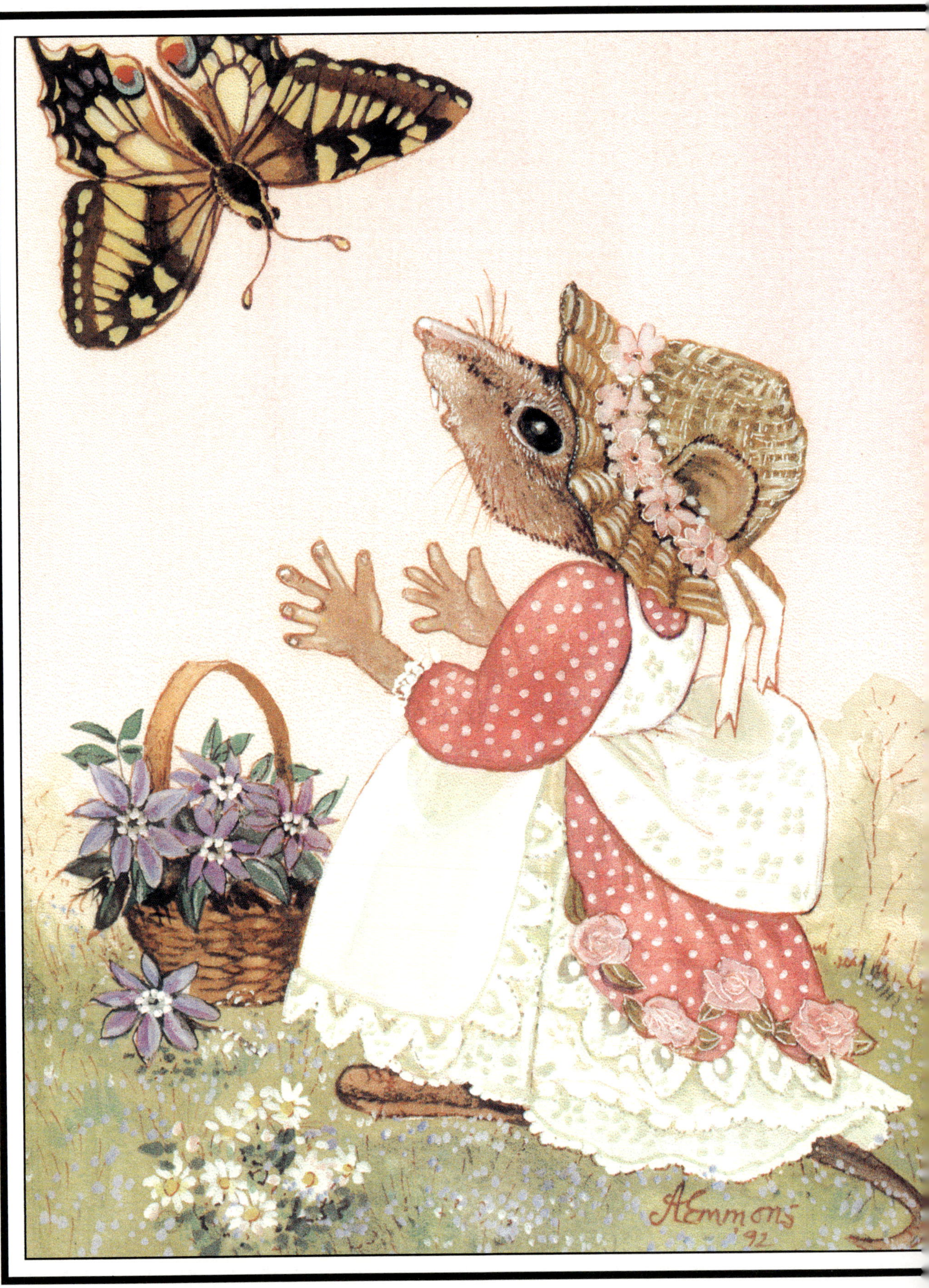
AEmmons
'92

BUTTERFLY

I cannot reach you
Butterfly
As you flit and flutter by
With painted wings of brilliant hue,
Like rainbows in a drop of dew.
Your time is short
So hurry on
For soon the Sunlight
Will be gone.
Flowers will close
Their nectar store,
The night will chill,
The wind will roar......
And you bright King
Will shine no more.

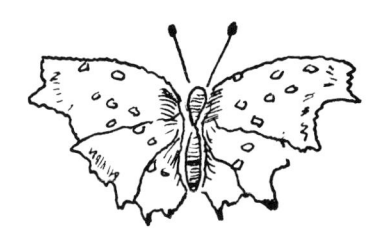

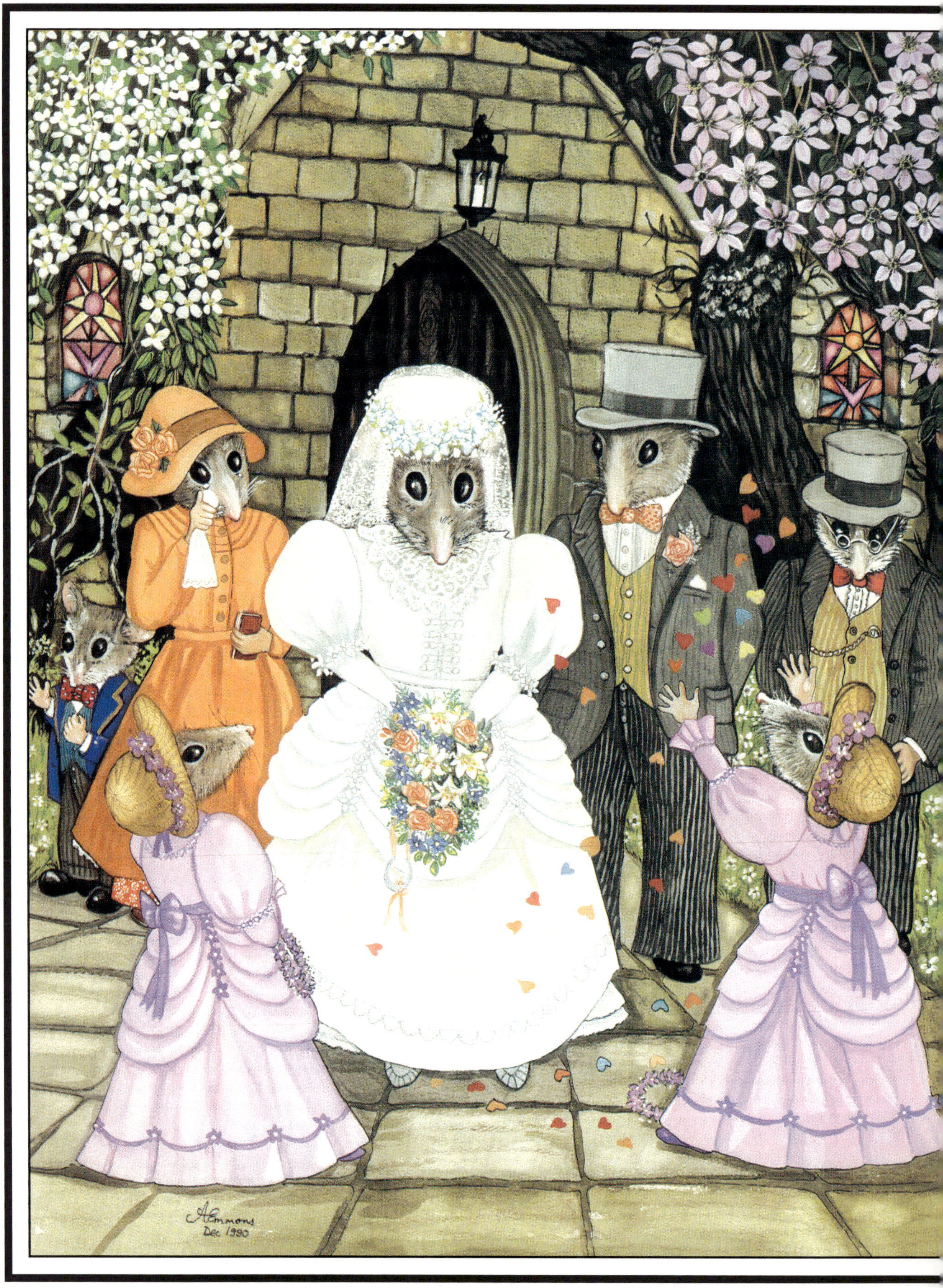
AEmmons
Dec 1990

WEDDING BELLS

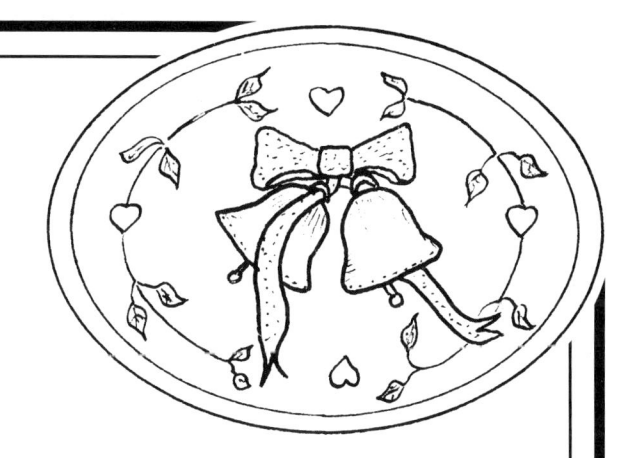

Let Wedding Bells ring
Loud and clear!
Give the Bride and Groom
A cheer!

The Bride is wearing Silk and Lace,
A radiant Smile upon her face.
Her Groom is just the sort
Of Mouse
She dreamt one day
Would be her Spouse.
Her Bridesmaids giggle
In a row,
All dressed in Satin
For the Show.

Her Mother weeps
Sad parting Tears,
Recalling all
The Happy Years.
But Pride and Joy
Are in her Eye
As with a Smile
She waves Goodbye.

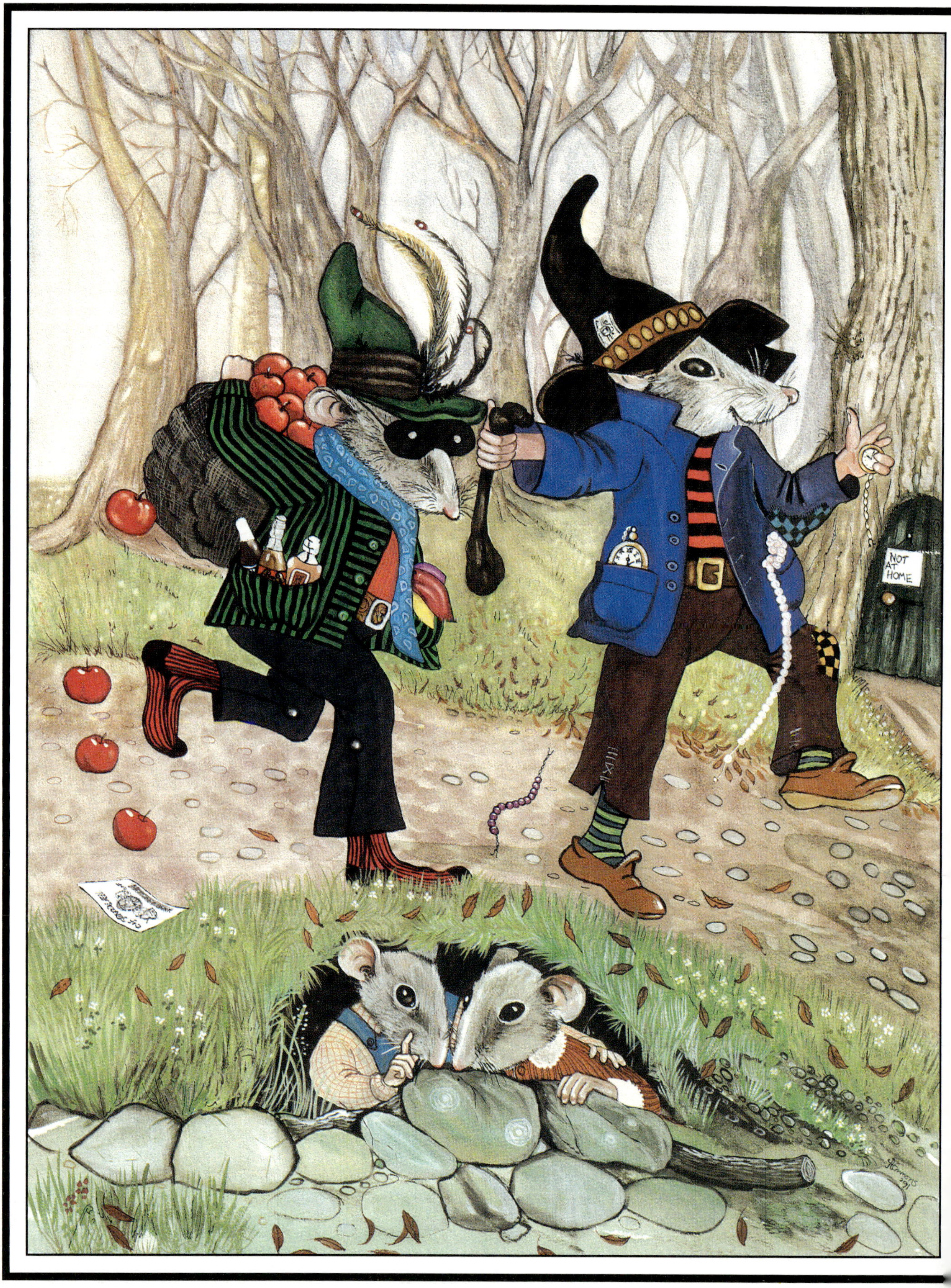
NOT AT HOME

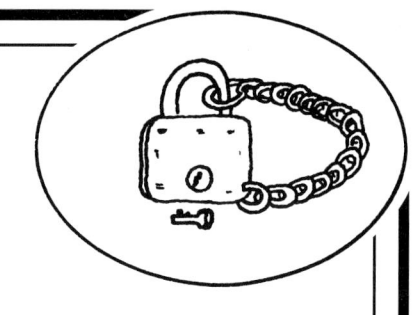

THE BRIGAND MICE

Be sure to bar your windows tight
And check your doors are locked tonight!
The Brigand Mice are on their way.
Let us pray they do not stay!

They are a most dishevelled crew
Of tinkers, tramps and robbers too,
Fearing no one, daring all,
They're ever ready for a brawl.

They steal the apples from your trees
In just the time it takes to sneeze!
Raiding larders! Looting cellars!
They plunder homes of country dwellers!

Dancing to a pipe and drum,
Shouting! Laughing! Here they Come!
Merry feet may shake the ground
But you and I will make no sound!

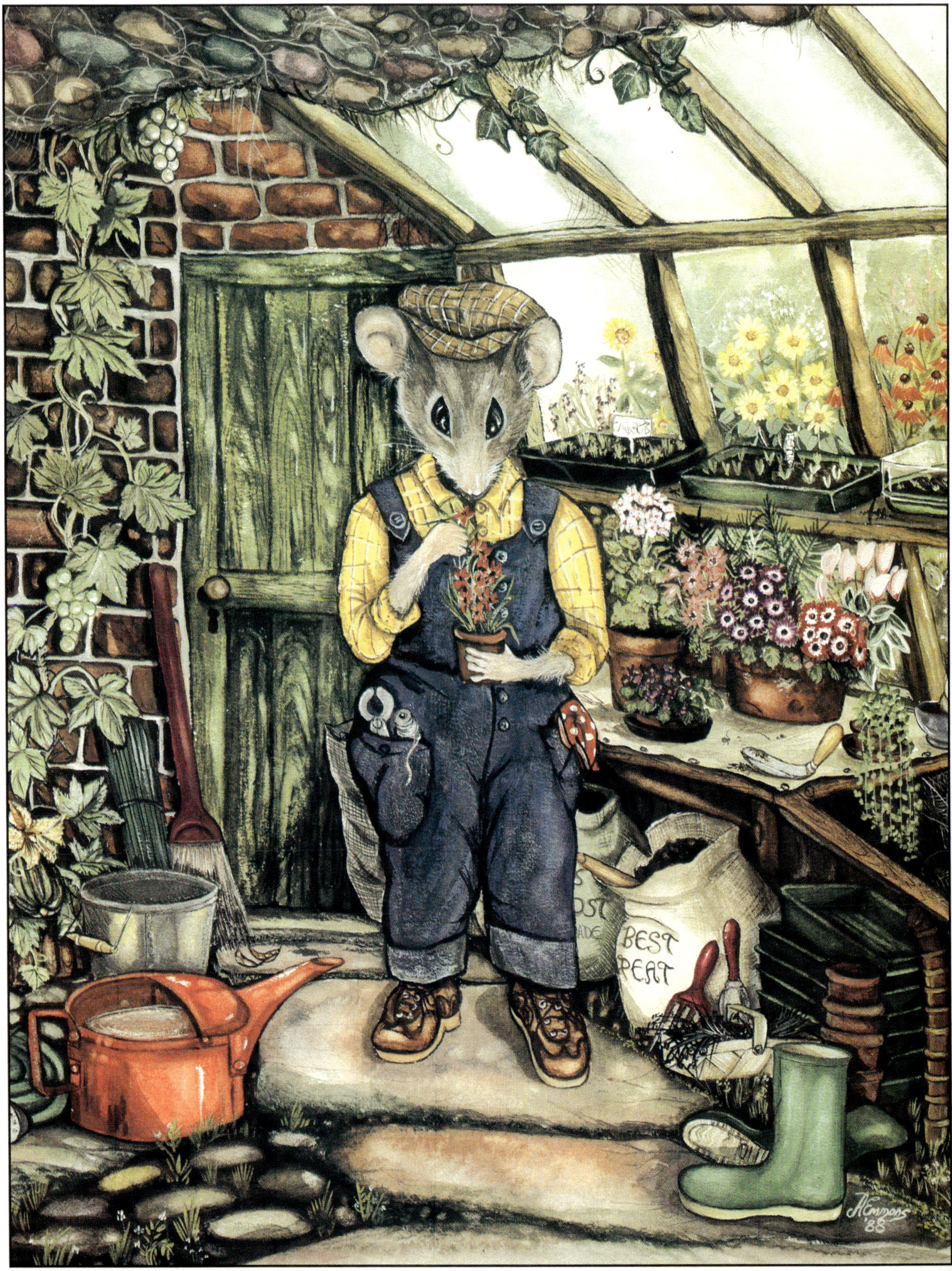
BEST
PEAT

MY UNCLE FRED

Out in the garden down in the shed
Is where you will find my Uncle Fred.
Potting pansies, sowing seeds,
Watering pot plants, pulling weeds.
Pruning his roses, trimming the hedge,
Setting his cuttings and growing his veg.
He's out in all weathers and all times of day,
Humming a tune as he's working away.

Now up at the house lives my old Aunt Clara,
Grandma Sybil and Cousin Sarah.
They like things clean, like things neat,
Hate the sight of muddy feet.
They squabble and gossip all day long,
Deciding what's right, sure of who's wrong.
And Uncle Fred says he will not stay
To spoil their chatter in any way.

So down to the potting shed he must go
Away from trouble and strife and woe.
And here with his plants he stays unseen
Passing the time in a peaceful dream.

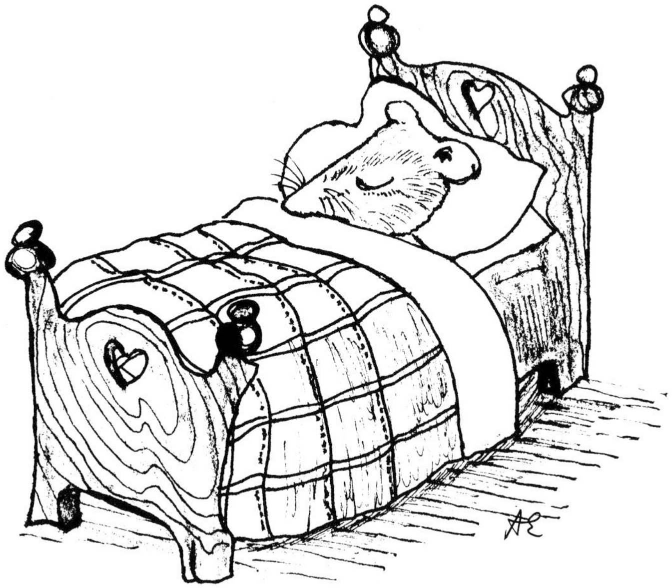

THOMAS MOUSE LOST

Thomas Mouse is Lost
Far from home,
With nowhere to rest his head.
Thomas Mouse hungry
And Oh so tired
Is dreaming of his own small bed.

Thomas Mouse rests,
Far from home
At the foot of an Old Oak Tree.
Thomas Mouse sighs
And almost cries
As he thinks of his family.

Thomas Mouse is found
Far from home
By his Mother and Uncle Fred.
They hug him and kiss him
Then take him home
And put him in his own small bed.

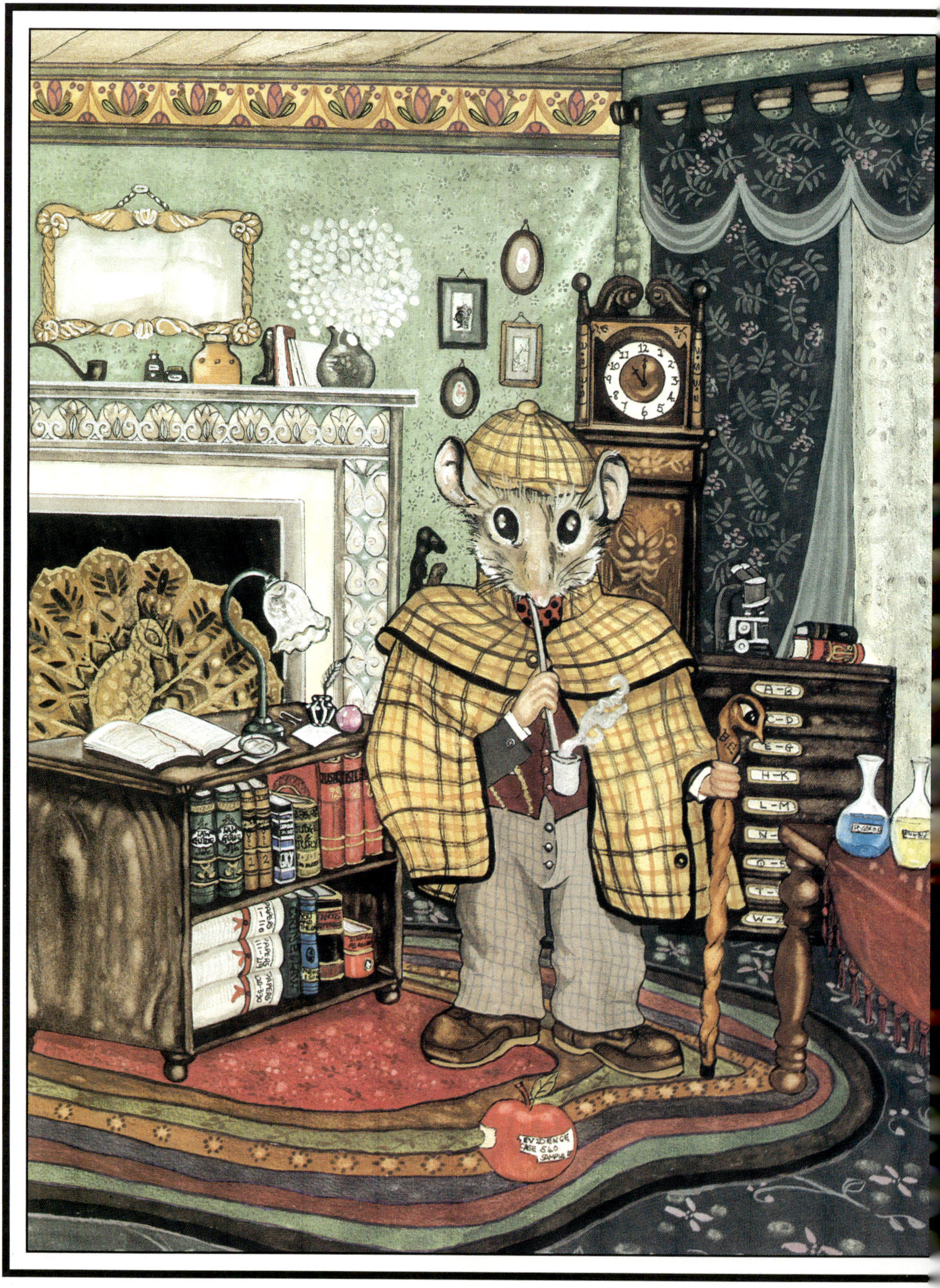
A-B
C-D
E-G
H-K
L-M

SIR BASIL EYE, DETECTIVE MOUSE

Sir Basil Eye, Detective Mouse,
The sleuth who solves the Crime,
Has cracked the hardest Cases
In the minimum of time.
He always finds the missing Link
That no one else can spot,
Outwitting Master Criminals
By seeing through their Plot.

He sifts through all the Evidence,
Examines every Clue,
Cross questions every Witness
To check their Statement's true.
And when he looks at Anyone
He seems to seek much more.
Could they be really innocent
Or would they break The Law?

He solved the Missing Cheeses Case,
And sent the villains down,
Caught Apple thieves Red-Handed
And chased them out of Town.
He found The Phantom Tail Puller,
Unmasked him on the spot,
And proved the bloodstain by The Well
Was just an old ink Blot.

And so you see what Great Deeds
Sir Basil Eye can do.
And if you seek his services
He might help you.

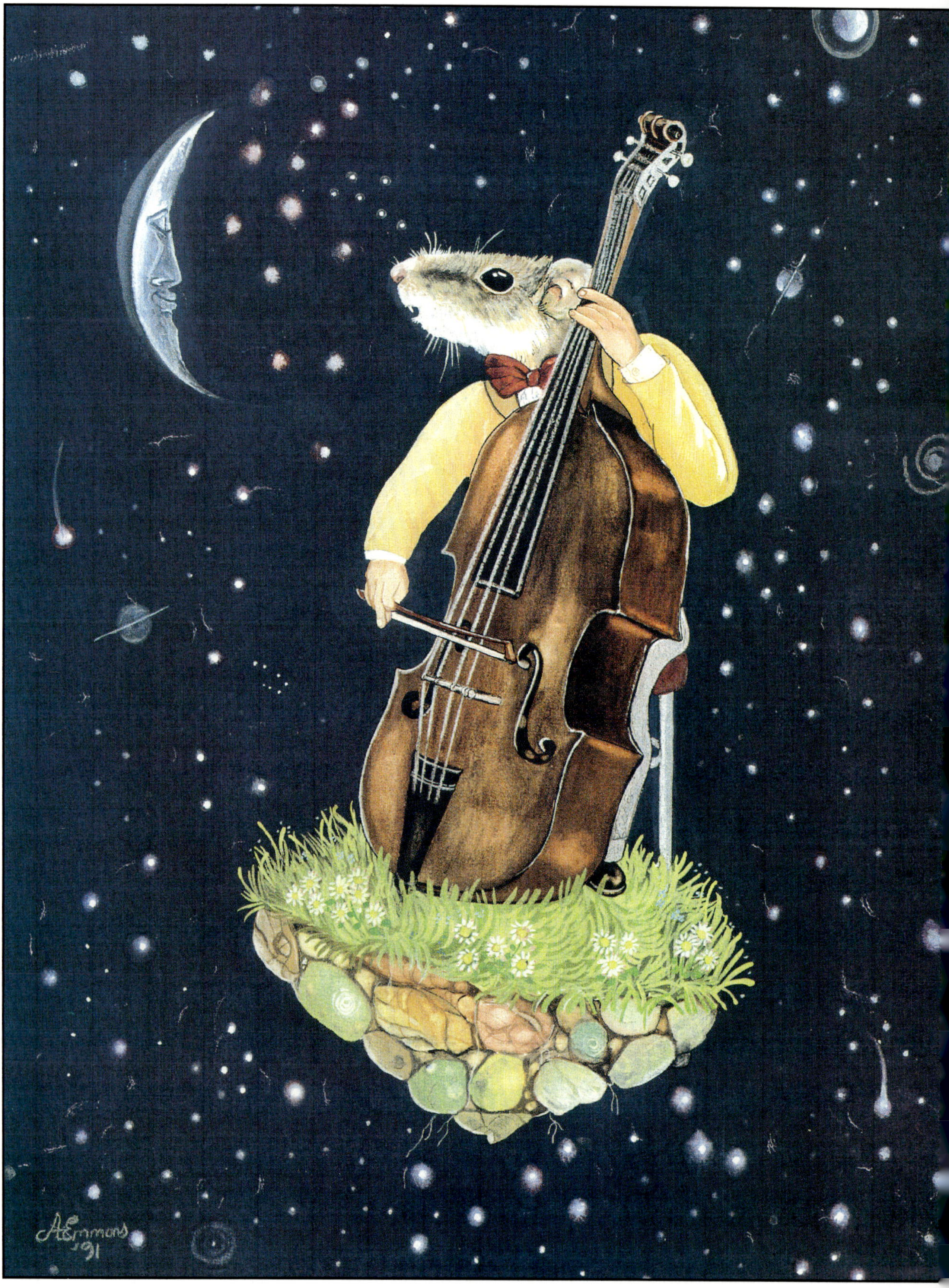
AEmmons
91

TO PLAY A DOUBLE BASS

To Play a Double Bass
Deep in Space,
To serenade the Stars
And hear them Sing,
To play the Crescent Moon
A Sentimental Tune
Would be a Wondrous Thing!

To watch the Comets Whirl
And the planets Twirl,
And the Sun Dance
In the Dark
Is a fantasy I Chase
As I play my Double Bass
On the bandstand in the Park.

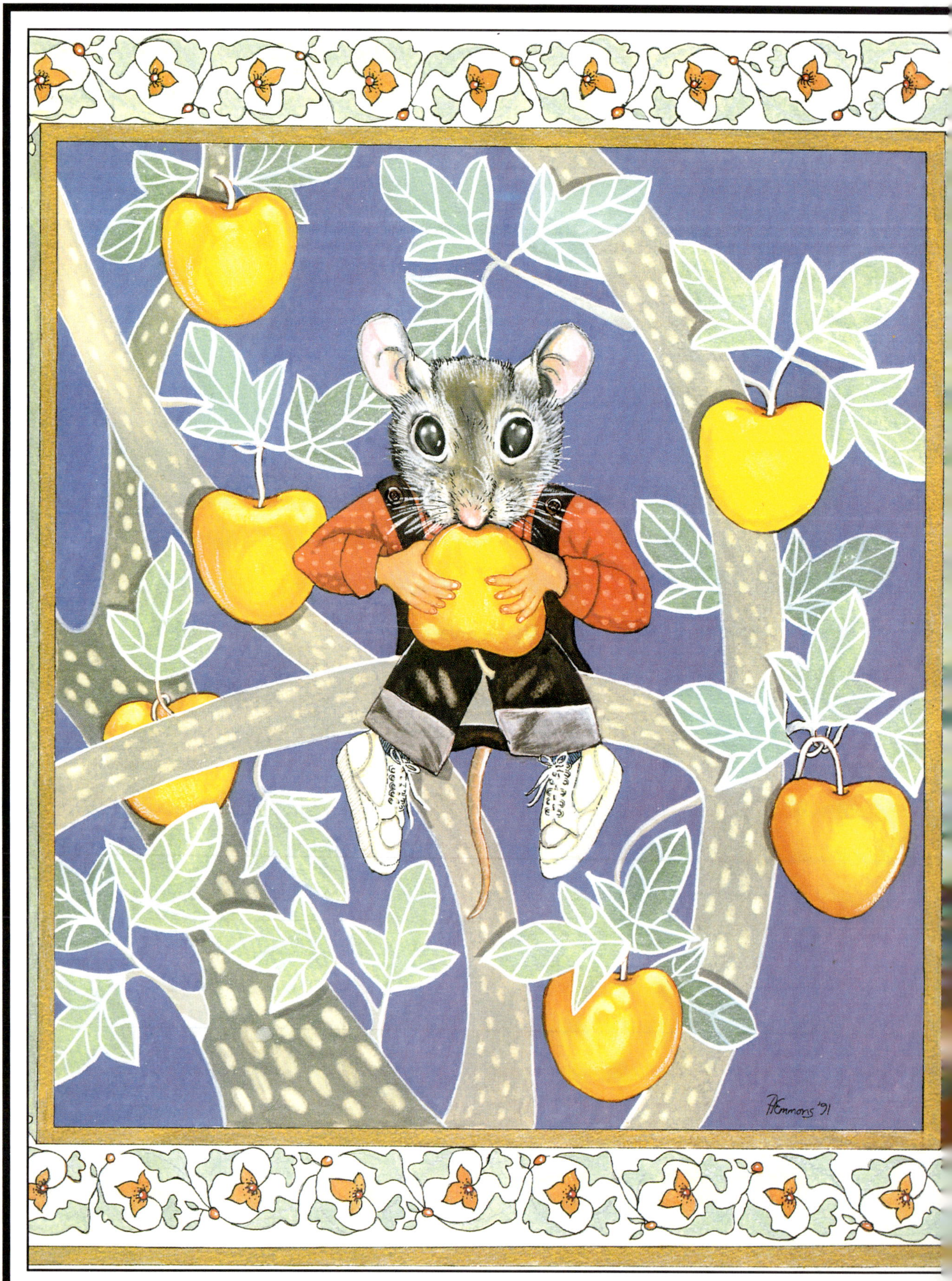

THE PARADISE TREE

Come and See
The Paradise Tree
Growing down our Lane.
Its leaves are Silver
As the Moon,
Its blossoms smell
Of Rich Perfume.
The fruit it bears
Is coloured Gold,
Large and Lovely
To behold,
Tasting of Sweet Summer Wine,
How I wish it could be mine!

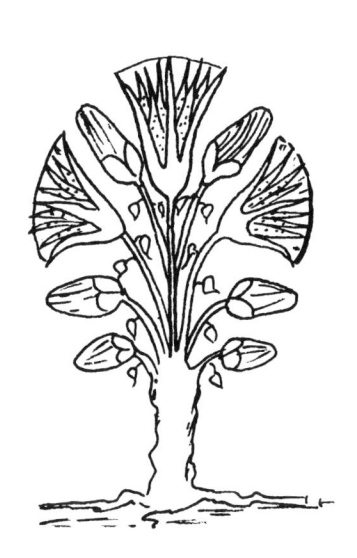

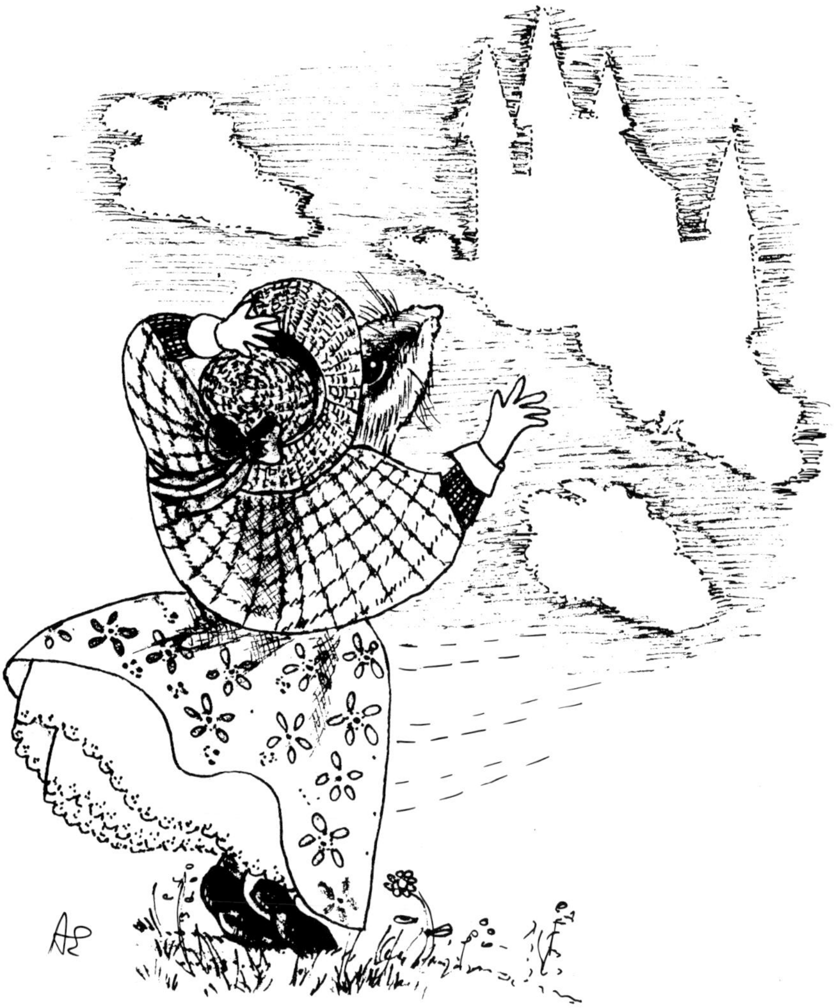

CASTLES IN THE AIR

See the Clouds go racing by
On a Windy day in a busy sky.
Watch them billow as they blow
Sails of Satin, White as Snow.
Where the clouds fly High and Free
Earth bound Mice can never be.
They can only stand and stare
At those Castles in the Air.

98

THE DREAMSPINNER

Above the highest Mountains
Beyond the cloudy sky
The Dreamspinner is watching
The World go whirling by.
He keeps a bag of Dreamdust
Ready by his side,
And throws it by the fistful
The stormy winds to ride.

It flutters down in sparkling showers
Spinning as it falls,
Disguised as dew on Spiders' webs
Or frost on garden walls.
But if it touches children
Who've just been sent to bed
It takes them to some other place
They'd rather go instead.

Perhaps they visit fun fairs
Where all the rides are free,
Or visit Islands far away
Beyond the Silvery Sea.
Or travel through great jungles
Seeking hidden gold
Or ride on horseback brave and proud
With warriors of old.

It only lasts a night time,
As every real dream should.
And dream dust never ever works
On children who aren't good!

PETUNIA MOUSE

Petunia Mouse, the Teacher's pet,
Has a charming smile you can't forget,
Impeccable manners, speech so fine
Considering that she's only nine.
She's so well groomed and very trim
In her blue school bonnet with scarlet rim.
Her shoes are polished sparkling bright,
Her socks are always clean and white.
She reads so clearly, writes so well,
Can sing and sew, do sums and spell.
And this, Dear Reader, lets you see
What a perfect pupil she must be!

But all these virtues irritate
Her fellow pupils in Class Eight,
For in Petunia they have spied
A not so pleasant hidden side.
They say her smile your heart will win
But really it's a cheeky grin.
Beneath her bonnet dark thoughts lurk
Which make her titter, gloat and smirk.
And at her desk behind her books
She gives the Teacher horrid looks.
She mimics Miss Bell all the time
With priggish voice and foolish whine.

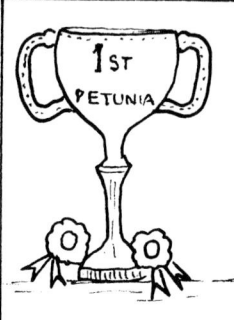

Petunia Mouse, the Perfect Pest,
Just causes trouble for the rest.
She pinches mice to make them cry
Then blames another passer by.
She makes mice quarrel, even fight,
By telling tales that aren't quite right.
She pulls their tails then runs away
And hides their toys so they can't play.
She's careful that she's never caught
Doing what she never ought,
So when the other Mice complain
The Teacher says she's not to blame!

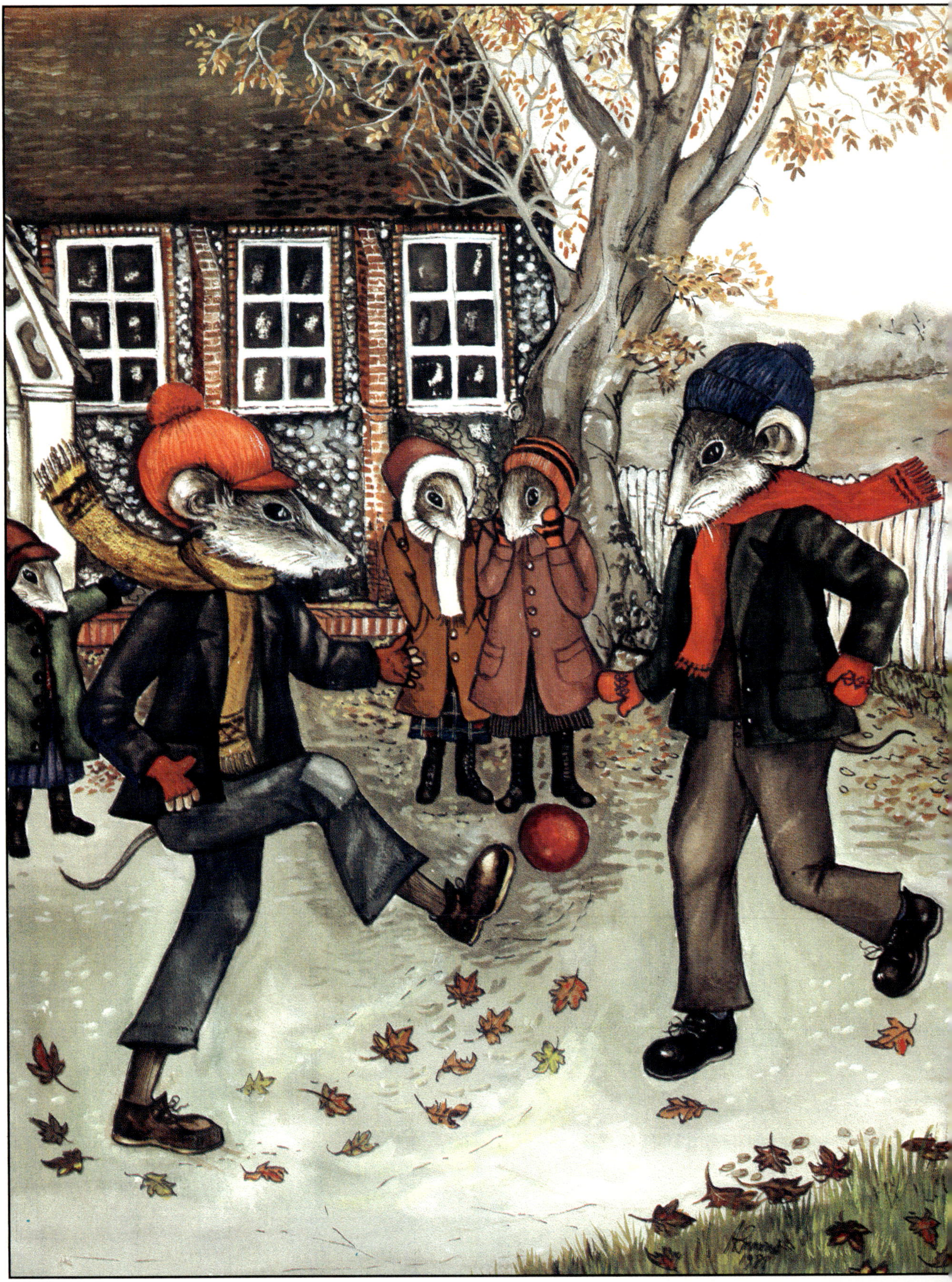

PLAYTIME

Put your pens and books away
And come outside so we can play.
Can't you see the weather's fine?
Join us in a merry time.
Bring your bat and ball and hoop
Play at planes and loop the loop.
Run and hide and skip along
Dance and sing a silly song.
Hopscotch, Marbles, All fall Down,
Act the Goat and play the Clown.
Put your worries all away
And save them for a rainy day.

104

COME WITH ME

Come with me to the fields of Spring
Where the new lambs dance and the young birds sing.
Where fragile blossoms blow sweet on the breeze,
And surging sap wakes the sleeping trees,
Where life is longing to be seen
And Nature's gown is green.

Come with me to the Summer fields
Where the corn grows ripe for the harvest yields.
Where poppies close with the setting sun,
And bees toil on till day is done,
And myriad colour blooms unfold
But Nature's gown is gold.

Come with me to the Autumn fields
Where the harvester his sickle wields.
Where swallows gather to start for home,
And leaves grow pale, ochre and chrome,
They tremble and then tumble down
And Nature's gown is brown.

Come with me to the Winter fields
Where Earth her children from harsh Frost shields.
Where spiked grass glistens crystal cold
And days grow short as the year grows old.
Grey is the mist and black the night
But Winter's gown is white.

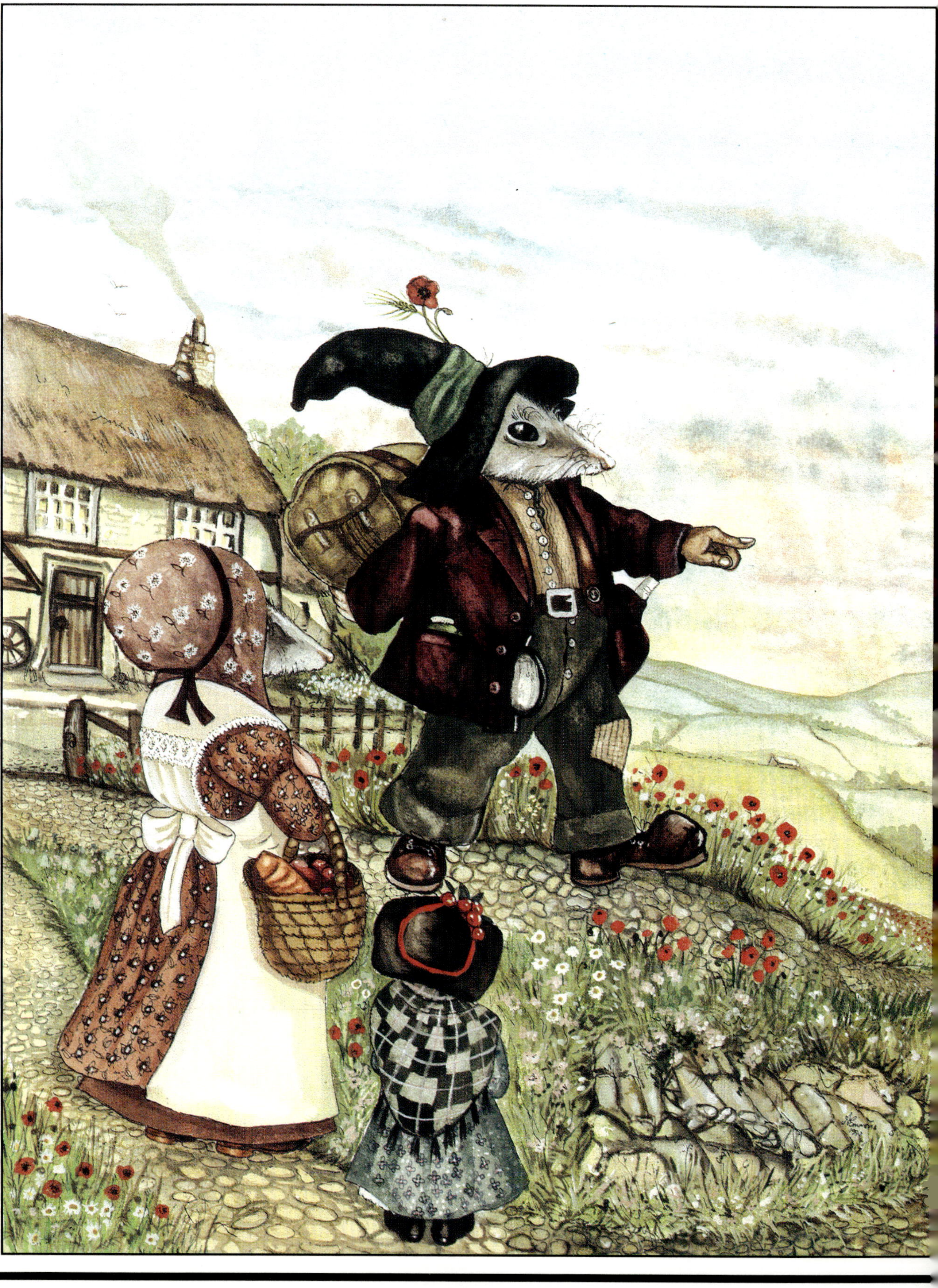

WHERE ARE YOU GOING?

"Where are you going to Master Mouse
And why do you hurry so,
With that heavy pack upon your back
Which makes you stoop so low?"

"I travel beyond the farthest hill,
Beyond the setting sun,
Where the sky meets land in palest hue
And Earth and Air are one."

"Stay awhile poor Master Mouse,
Our fire is warm and bright.
We'll give you broth and ale and bread
And rest and cheer this night."

"I thank you but I cannot stay,
The road goes on and on
And I must take it all the way
And hesitate for none.
For when I reach the twilight
You see beyond the hill
Night will hide the way from me
But I must travel still."

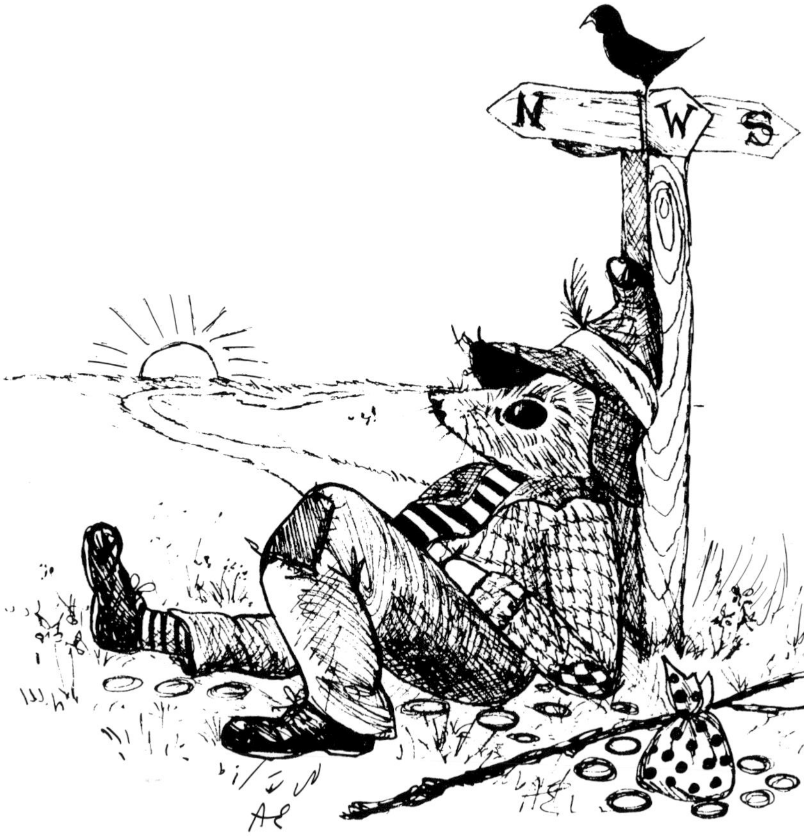
N
W
S

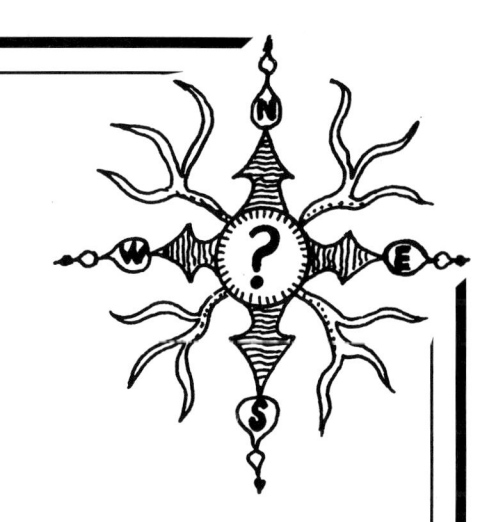

THE CROSSROADS

North, South, East, West,
Which way shall I go?
For any path I take will lead
Somewhere I do not know.

The North path is a dark Path
Deep in the Forest's shade,
The South path is a steep Path
O'er craggy hilltops laid.

The Eastern Path meanders,
The Western path is Straight,
Towards the Sunrise or Sunset,
Which way will be my fate?

Maybe at the Crossroads
Is where I'll choose to stay.
Who needs to make decisions
On such a lovely day?

110

WINTER'S NIGHT

It's ten o'clock and here we are
Tucked up and warm in bed.
We've locked the door on old Jack Frost,
On howling wind forlorn and lost,
To let the Black Night creep on by
While we lie ready, snug and dry
Soon to Slumberland to fly.

Our bed just like a little boat
Will float away on dreams,
And travel to some Wonderland
We see but cannot understand,
Where all that glistens is real gold,
Where Elf Folk live their legends old
And where there is no biting cold.

But far from slumber hoots the owl,
Hunter of the night.
Piercing dreams with deepest fear,
Sounds of danger drawing near
Rattle the door and windows thin,
But have no fear they can't get in
Beyond the dream world that we spin.

112

DOCTOR AMOS PERIWINKLE

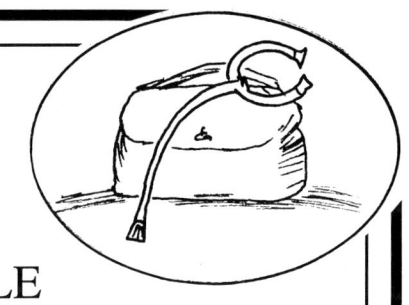

Doctor Amos Periwinkle
That mouse of High Degree,
Knew all about Biology
When he was only three.
He took a country practice
From dear old Doctor Bell
And spent his time rewardingly
Making Rich Folk well.
He had no end of patience
With Patients who could pay,
But all the humble Country Folk
He simply turned away.

One day a dreadful Tragedy
This Charlatan befell,
As lightning struck the Practice
And 'Oak Tree Cottage' fell.
Amos had nowhere to go,
No desk, no chair, no bed.
His patients sent their sympathy,
Then went to Town instead.
He begged for help from all around,
But little did he find,
For humble Country Folk are poor,
And not the giving kind.

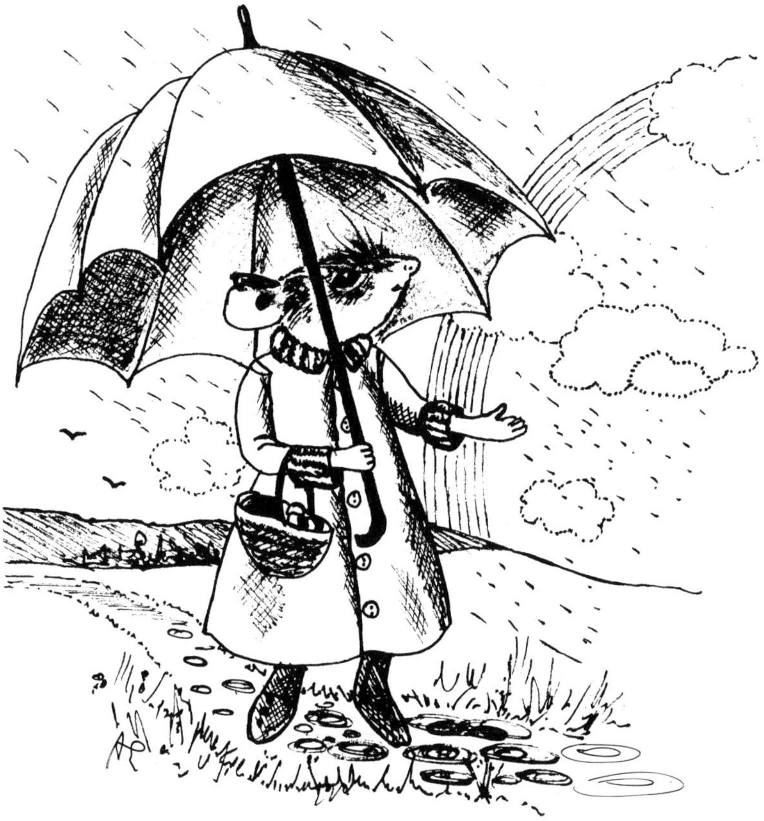

THE WEATHER SHOW

Where does the Rainbow go?
Why does the Wild Wind blow?
Why does the Snow fall when it's cold?
How can a Sunset turn to Gold?
Why, when the Sky turns black as Night
Does Thunder roar and Lightning strike?
Why does the Rain come tumbling down
Where Tiny Things can fall and drown?
Why does the Hail cut through the Air
And spoil the Flowers everywhere?

The rainbow goes to Earth,
In light it has its Birth.
The Wild Wind wanders free
For No one's fool is he.
The snow falls pure and white
To brighten Winter's Night.
And Sunsets may turn Gold
When Sunny Days grow old.
Raindrops feed the Flowers
And Sunshine warms the Showers.
But Thunder, Hail and Lightning
Are Frightening and Exciting
And aim to let you know
They Rule The Weather Show.

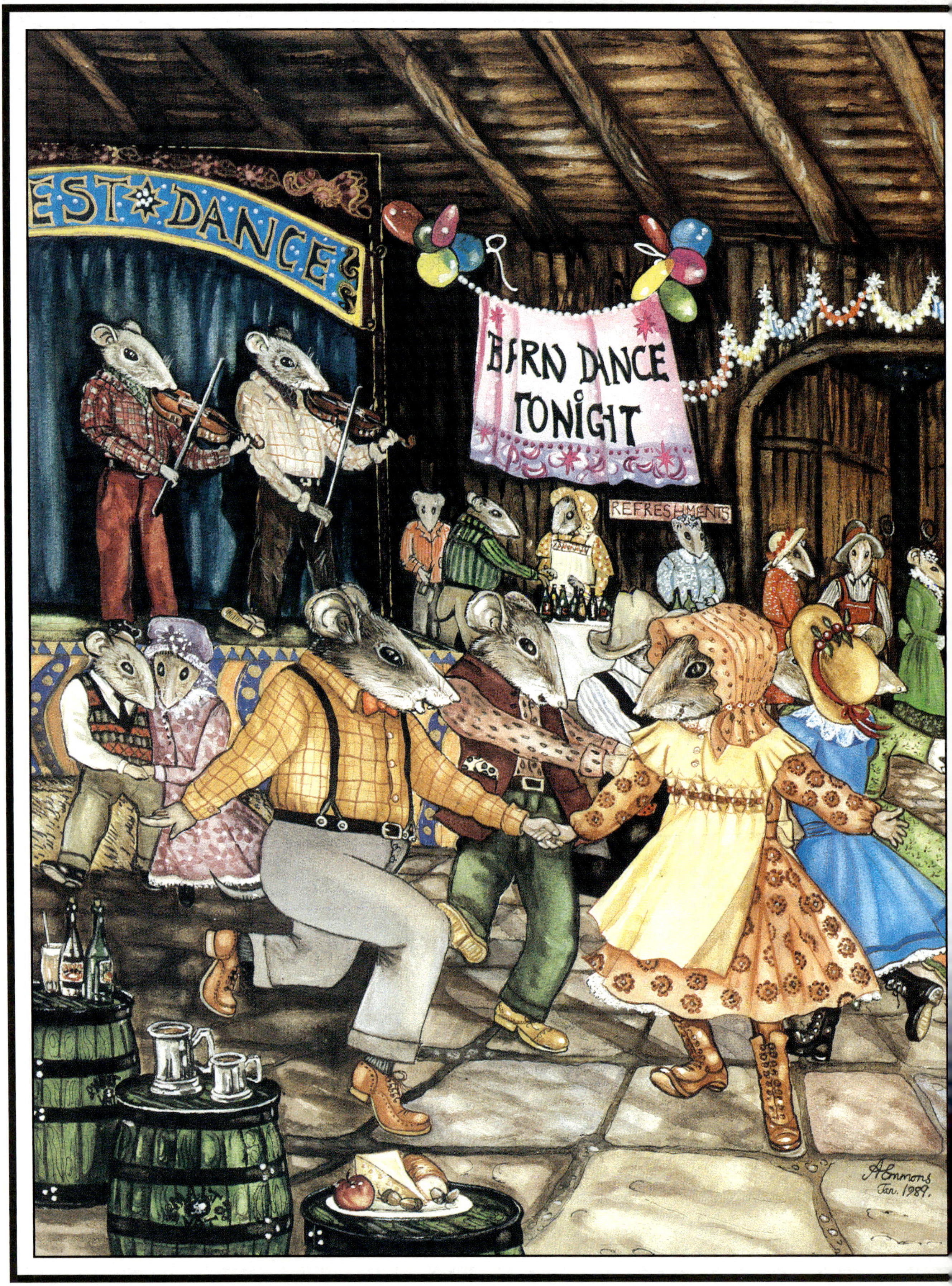
BARN DANCE
TONIGHT
REFRESHMENTS

COME TO THE BARN DANCE TONIGHT

Take your partners,
Circle round
So your feet
Don't touch the ground.
Do-si-do
Your corner girl
Clap your hands
And do a twirl.

Everyone is
Here tonight,
Having fun
And feeling bright.
Tall ones, short ones,
Fat and thin,
Dancing to
The violin.

Grab that girl
With the sunny smile,
Skip with her
Right down the aisle.
Swing her fast
And swing her high,
Kiss her once
Then pass her by.

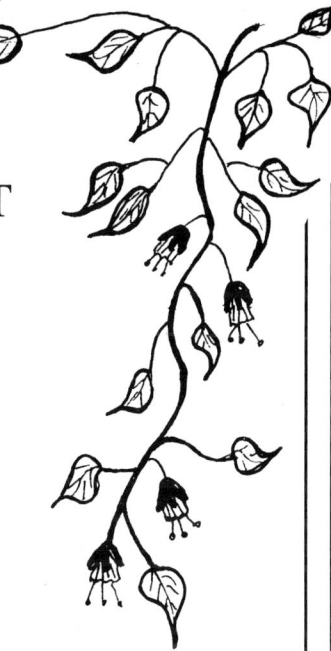

118

CANDY CHERRIES

Shall we bake
For us to eat
A really special
Tea-time treat?
A cake with sugar
Eggs and flour
Baked in the oven
Half an hour.
Covered with icing
Dripping down
With Candy Cherries
For its crown.

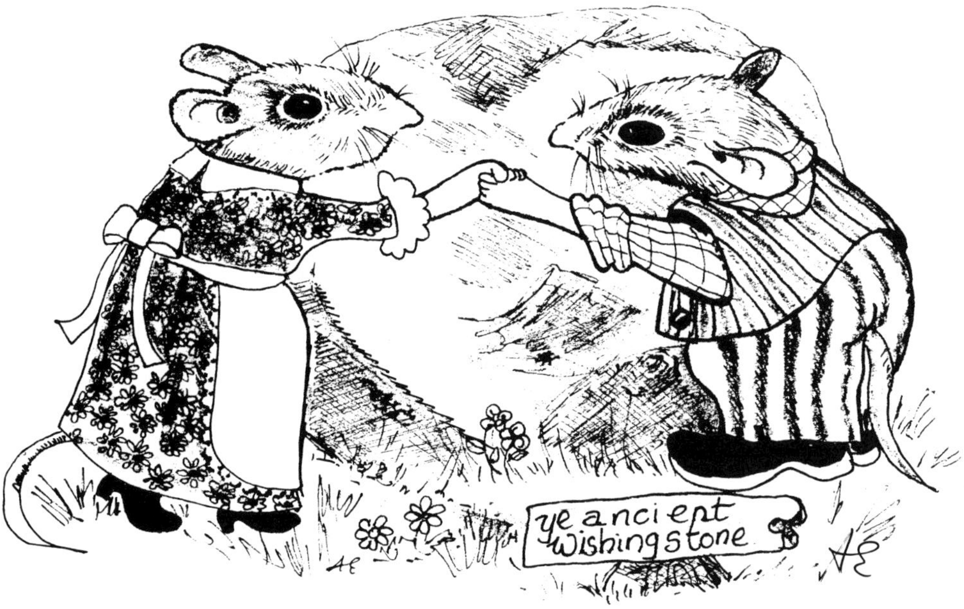
ye ancient
wishingstone

THE WISHING STONE

Forever and Ever there has been
A Wishing Stone on the Village Green.
No one knows from whence it came,
But it well deserves its name.

Secrets silently it holds,
Hopes and Aspirations bold,
Whispered by the little Mice
Casting dreams and wishes thrice.

And their wishes do come true,
Something special, something New,
Cheers their hearts and chases fear
Keeps them happy all the year.

122

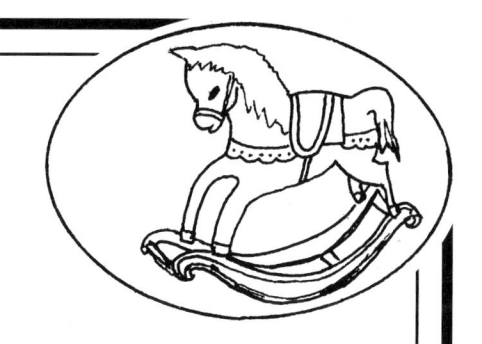

THE ROCKING HORSE

"Rocking Horse, Rocking Horse, where would you ride
Free from the nursery far outside?
Where would you take us that we've not been?
What could you show us we have not seen?"

"I'd take you back to a far off land
Where stallions gallop on silvery sand
And mares of white ride the deep blue sky
And grass is green and lush and high."

"Dear Rocking Horse we can no longer ride
On your worn out saddle and dappled hide
The world of the nursery soon must change
For another world that's new and strange."

"I'll never forget you but will not grieve
When the door locks fast as you take your leave
For there at the window I can see
A snow white mare who's come for me."

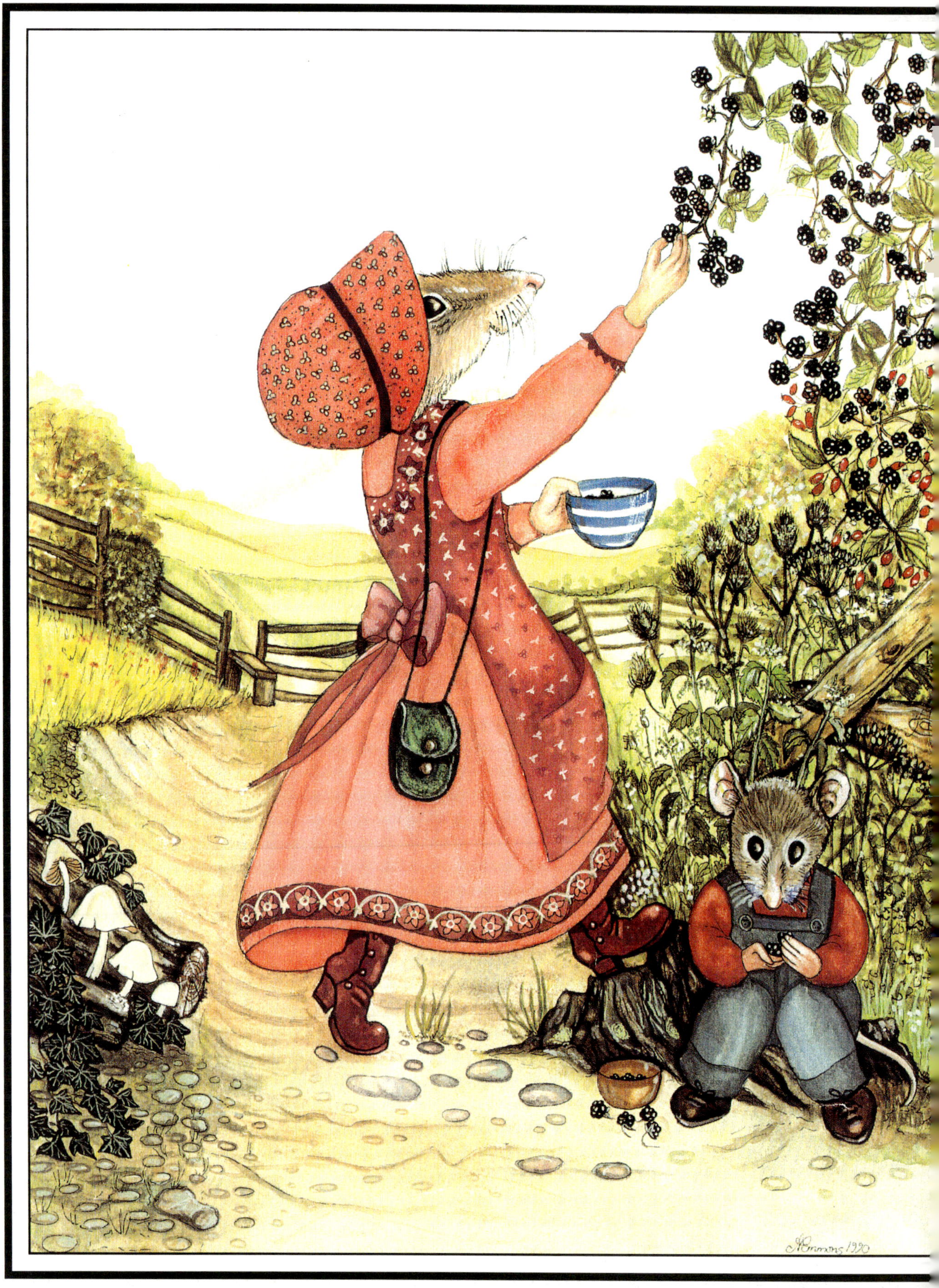

BLACKBERRIES RIPE

Blackberries Ripe
Juicy and Sweet,
Pick you we must
For our Harvest Treat.
Long before Frost
Makes you shrivel and die
We'll turn you into
Blackberry Pie.

Ruby red Hips,
The fruit of the Rose,
Pick you we must
As the Summer goes.
Syrup we'll make,
And Rose Hip Tea,
Rich and Amber,
Served with Honey.

Sad Elderberries,
Don't droop and pine.
Pick you we must
For our Winter's Wine.
Folk say the Elder
Keeps Witches at bay,
So good health to blossoms
That bear you next May.

126

THE GHOST

There's a ghost on the stair
I know he's there!
There's a ghost on the stair
But I don't care.
I'm in bed all warm and snug,
While he's sitting out on the landing rug.
He can rattle the handle of my bedroom door,
But I'll ignore him and pretend to snore.
He can leer through the keyhole with his ugly
   face,
I know his manners are a big disgrace.
He can't get in, there is no way,
So he'll soon get bored and go away.

There's a ghost on the stair,
Hear him howl!
Like the moaning wind,
Like the screeching owl.
He wants to come in and say 'Hello',
But the door is locked, so he might as well go.

There's a ghost on the stair,
It's my silly brother.
With a sheet on his head
That he's pinched from mother.

ACKNOWLEDGEMENTS

Paintings reproduced by kind permission of :-

Mr and Mrs H Scott
Mrs P. Wilkinson
Mr and Mrs K. De Turberville
Mr and Mrs B. Court
Mr J. Burton
Mr and Mrs R. Nuttall
Mr and Mrs C. Harwood
Mr and Mrs Hutchings
Mr P. Wiesendanger
Mr and Mrs D. Pearce
Mrs J. Coffey
Mrs A. Prince
Mr R. Stone

INDEX TO COLOUR PLATES

The Mice Of Lardon Hill 8
Pedlar Peg 12
The Flower Seller 18
The Garden Wall 22
Where The Mermaids Sing 34
Starlight 42
The Field Mouse And The Fairy 46
Story Time 54
Madam Phoebe 62
O Little Town 70
Abigail The Witch Mouse 76
Wedding Bells 82
My Uncle Fred 86
To Play A Double Bass 92
The Dreamspinner 98
Come With Me 104
Winter's Night 110
Come To The Barn Dance Tonight 116
The Rocking Horse 122

The Hermit Mouse 10
Who Is Out ? 16
Miss Moffat 20
Abdul The Magician 30
Summer's Here 36
How Far Away Is Fairyland ? 44
Echo In The Breeze 52
Market Day 60
Miss Juniper Mouse 68
Miss Bustle, Miss Bark And Miss Bell 74
Butterfly 80
The Brigand Mice 84
Sir Basil Eye, Detective Mouse 90
The Paradise Tree 94
Playtime 102
Where Are You Going ? 106
Dr Amos Periwinkle 112
Candy Cherries 118
Blackberries Ripe 124